# CYCLING THE CANAL DU MIDI

## About the Author

Declan Lyons brings a lifelong passion for cycling and touring to this guide. He was bitten by the bug when, as a teenager in the 1960s, he explored the wilds of Connemara on a rusty three-speed Rudge bicycle. Since then he has toured extensively in Ireland and further afield. He's cycled throughout France, including regular trips from the Channel to the Mediterranean.

You can see the plane trees bordering the Canal du Midi from Declan's home in Portiragnes. He has spent the past decade exploring its history, culture and wildlife by bike – accompanied by his wife, son and fellow enthusiasts.

# CYCLING THE CANAL DU MIDI

**by
Declan Lyons**

2 POLICE SQUARE, MILNTHORPE, CUMBRIA LA7 7PY
www.cicerone.co.uk

© Declan Lyons 2009
First edition 2009
ISBN: 978 1 85284 559 9

A catalogue record for this book is available from the British Library.
All photographs are by the author unless otherwise stated.

*This guide is dedicated to the memory of Tom O'Driscoll –
friend, colleague, runner and cyclist.*

### Acknowledgements

Special thanks are due to Ms Veruschka Becquart of the French Government Tourist Office for her help in researching this guide. Thanks also to the staff of Voies Navigables de France (VNF) for the valuable information that they supplied. My wife Mary, our son Oscar and my brother-in-law Michael accompanied me on parts of the route and I thank them for their advice and support throughout the project. Mary deserves special thanks for her great help and encouragement during the writing of the guide. Thanks too for the help and guidance from the Cicerone team of Jonathan Williams, Lois Sparling, Sue Viccars and Caroline Draper.

### Advice to Readers
Readers are advised that, while every effort is taken by the author to ensure the accuracy of this guidebook, changes can occur which may affect the contents. It is advisable to check locally on such things as transport, accommodation and shops but even rights of way can be altered.
The publisher would welcome notes of any such changes.

*Front cover:* Boating on the Canal du Midi

# CONTENTS

**INTRODUCTION** .................................................................. 9
Regions of the canal ............................................................. 10
Why by bike? ..................................................................... 11
When to cycle .................................................................... 12
How to use this guide ........................................................... 15
History ........................................................................... 16
The construction of the canal .................................................. 23
Culture: festivals and sport .................................................... 25

**PRACTICALITIES** ............................................................... 27
Getting there and getting around .............................................. 27
Your bike ......................................................................... 30
Health and safety ................................................................ 32
Accommodation .................................................................. 39
Eating and drinking ............................................................. 41
Packing ........................................................................... 44
Money, phones and email ....................................................... 46

**THE ROUTE**
| | | |
|---|---|---|
| **Stage 1** | Toulouse to Port Lauragais | 47 |
| **Stage 2** | Port Lauragais to Carcassone | 65 |
| | *Excursion:* from Guerre lock to St-Férréol reservoir | 79 |
| **Stage 3** | Carcassone to Homps | 84 |
| | *Excursion:* from Trèbes to Lastours | 93 |
| | *Excursion:* from Homps to Minerve | 98 |
| **Stage 4** | Homps to Béziers | 104 |
| | *Excursion:* to Narbonne and Port la Nouvelle | 124 |
| **Stage 5** | Béziers to Sète | 137 |
| | *Excursion:* to Vendres salt lagoon | 154 |
| | *Excursion:* across Portiragnes marshes and to Séringnan | 160 |

| | | |
|---|---|---|
| **APPENDIX 1** | Stage planning table | 167 |
| **APPENDIX 2** | Accommodation | 168 |
| **APPENDIX 3** | Tourist offices | 181 |
| **APPENDIX 4** | English–French glossary | 182 |
| **APPENDIX 5** | Market days | 184 |
| **APPENDIX 6** | Bike repair shops | 186 |
| **APPENDIX 7** | Further reading | 187 |

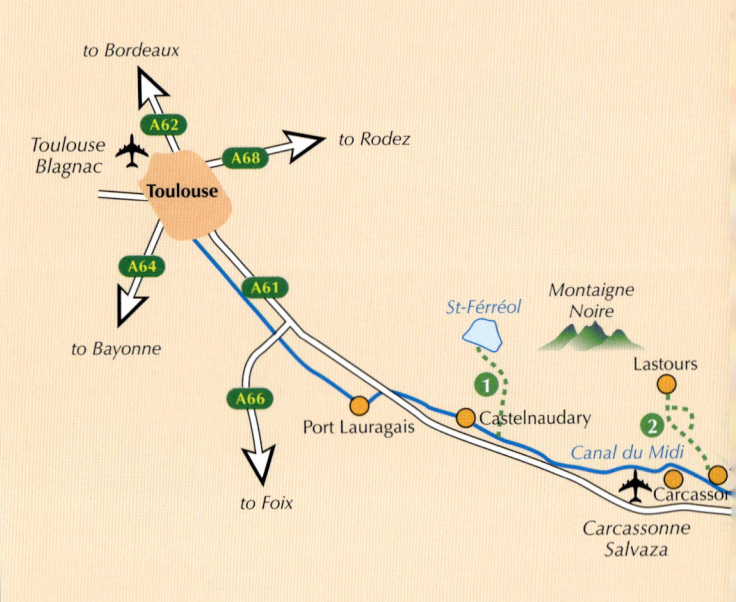

EXCURSIONS
1. Saint Férréol
2. Lastours
3. Minerve
4. Narbonne canal system
5. Vendres Salt Lagoon
6. Portiragnes Marsh

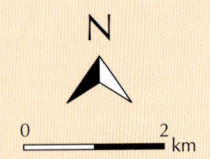

# Overview of the Canal du Midi and excursions

# Map Key

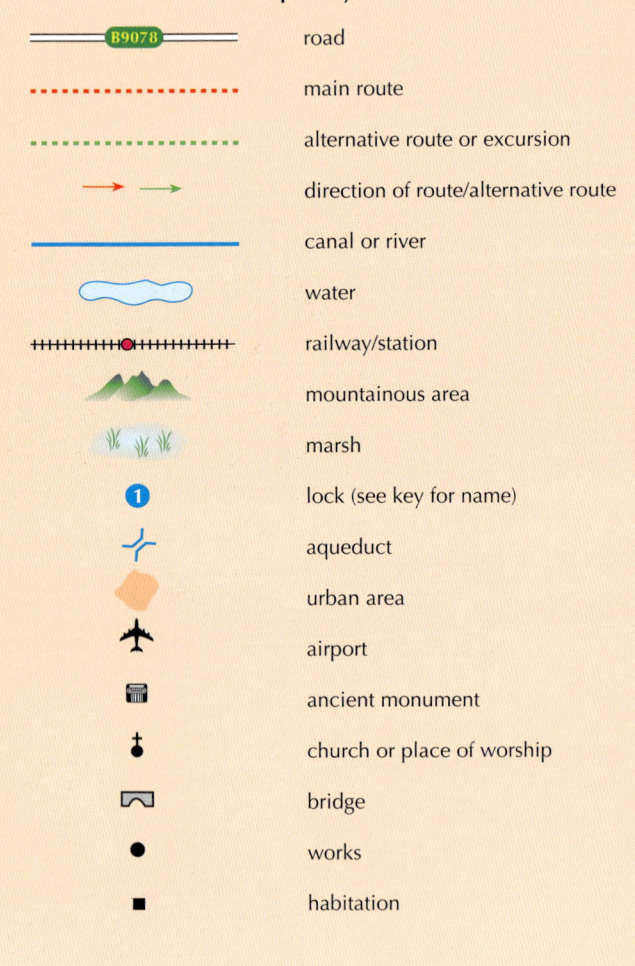

|  |  |
|---|---|
| ──B9078── | road |
| · · · · · · · · · · | main route |
| · · · · · · · · · · | alternative route or excursion |
| → → | direction of route/alternative route |
| ──────── | canal or river |
| 〰️ | water |
| ┼┼┼┼┼●┼┼┼┼┼ | railway/station |
| ⛰️ | mountainous area |
| 〰️ | marsh |
| ❶ | lock (see key for name) |
| ╬ | aqueduct |
| ▰ | urban area |
| ✈ | airport |
| 🏛 | ancient monument |
| ✝ | church or place of worship |
| ⌒ | bridge |
| ● | works |
| ■ | habitation |

# INTRODUCTION

La France Profonde – *deepest France*

On 13 April 1667 Pierre Paul Riquet began work on one of the world's best cycle tracks. It wasn't his intention; the bicycle had yet to be invented. He set out to construct a canal, the Canal du Midi, but the 240km towpath along its banks is now a cyclist's dream.

The canal's towpath, linking Toulouse in the Haute Garonne with Sète on the Mediterranean coast, is an excellent and rewarding cycle. It passes through some of France's most beautiful and historic countryside: rolling plains enlivened with sunflowers, dark mountain ranges, oak forests, tinder-dry *garigue*, Camargue-like marshland and sandy coastlines. The towns and villages which punctuate its route are steeped in history and culture. This area is part of *France Profonde* (anywhere in France where the rural way of life still prevails); the towns and villages feel authentic and you experience genuine French life.

It is hard to believe that the canal is manmade; it seems natural and fits perfectly into its surroundings. It's a thriving refuge and wildlife corridor for a wide range of animals and plants.

Riquet built the canal to enable goods to pass more quickly from Bordeaux, on the Atlantic, to the Mediterranean ports without boats having to circumnavigate the Iberian

Peninsula. This saved time and secured supplies in uncertain, turbulent times. Back then trade brought wealth as evidenced by the elegant buildings in older districts of the canal's towns, and today it still generates business. Tourist boats, walkers and cyclists have replaced the working barges, and the canal is a focal point for sporting and leisure activities.

Villages, towns and cities along the canal predate its construction. Ancient Greeks founded Agde and the Romans developed Narbonne. Toulouse, the 'Rose City', has been one of France's most beautiful and important cities for over one thousand years. Carcassonne's Cité is a restored 12th-century Cathar stronghold.

The arrival of railways in the late 19th century and the later construction of truck-carrying motorways undermined the economics of moving goods by barge. The Canal du Midi went into commercial decline, and the last commercial barges travelled it in 1970.

UNESCO declared the Canal du Midi a World Heritage Site in 1996, recognising its unique engineering heritage and its historic importance in the development of the Languedoc area in the south of France. It rates alongside France's great monuments such as the Eiffel Tower and the Popes' palaces in Avignon. The Canal du Midi is a working, almost living artefact. As you cycle its banks you can feel, touch and taste the history and culture of the area it enriches.

This book gives information on cycling the Canal du Midi from one end to the other. It is ideal for those who want to spend a holiday canal cycling, and will also be of interest to those living or holidaying in the region who are looking for a few days of good cycling.

Those boating down the canal will also find this guide useful; most of the boat-hire companies offer bicycles for hire. Cycling offers boat users the opportunity to explore the countryside that they pass through. Bikes give easy access to towns and villages at a short distance from the canal.

## REGIONS OF THE CANAL

The Canal du Midi is part of a waterway system linking the Atlantic Ocean with the Mediterranean Sea. Together, the River Garonne and the Canal Lateral link the Canal du Midi to the Atlantic in the west. It joins the Mediterranean at Sète. A spur of the Canal du Midi – the Canals de Jonction and de la Robine – connects it to Port la Nouvelle on the Mediterranean coast.

The canal flows through the French Midi-Pyrenees and Languedoc-Rousillon regions. Midi-Pyrenees is a combination of 'Midi' (meaning southern lands) and 'Pyrenees' (from the mountain range). Languedoc refers to the area where the Occitan (Oc) language was once spoken; 'oc' is Occitan for 'yes'. Rousillon was a

*Picking grapes near the canal*

Catalan principality. This name dates back to Roman times and comes from a fortified area called 'Ruscino' close to the French border with Catalonia. It is easy to be confused by the various names given to the region. Occitan was spoken far more widely than just the region now known as Languedoc-Rousillon. The language is closer to Catalan than French, and is taught in schools and in universities such as Toulouse.

France is also divided into 99 administrative departments, usually – although not always – named after the main river flowing through them. Each department has a number assigned in alphabetical order. The Canal du Midi passes through the Haute-Garonne (31), the Aude (11) and the Hérault (34), named after the rivers Garonne (*haute* referring to upper), the Aude and the Hérault. Cars display the relevant department number at the end of their registration.

## WHY BY BIKE?

France is one of the most cycling-friendly countries in the world. Up to 20 million French people cycle annually, and so much of the country is geared towards the activity. The Languedoc area is working hard to establish itself as the cycling holiday centre of France, and local authorities are expanding an already extensive network of cycle tracks. Some of these incorporate parts of the towpath and offer the cyclist an opportunity to explore surrounding countryside safely and easily.

## CYCLING THE CANAL DU MIDI

Towns and villages along the route go out of their way to welcome cyclists. Larger towns provide bicycle lock-ups or safe parking, and hotels usually have secure areas for bikes. Café owners won't bat an eyelid if you arrived smeared in grease or oil.

Cars are excluded from most of the towpath; roads are rural and relatively free of traffic. Plane trees shade most of the canal's length, giving some protection from the summer's sun and shelter in wetter weather.

It is easy to divide the cycle into manageable stages. There are plenty of stopping points, allowing you to pace yourself. Food, fresh water and accommodation are readily available close to the canal. Those looking for a greater challenge can make excursions into nearby mountains or explore forest and marsh tracks.

The canal is easy to access, with airports, train stations and motorways nearby. By air it takes a few hours to reach it from most of Europe's airports. It is under seven hours' drive from Paris and 11 hours from Calais. There are train stations along its length, and the French train service is becoming increasingly bike-friendly.

### WHEN TO CYCLE

One of the great attractions of the Canal du Midi is that it can be cycled throughout the year. There are times, however, when the weather is more

*Respect other users*

# WHEN TO CYCLE

*Fruit is abundant in summer*

reliable and the experience is more pleasant. I've cycled the route in all seasons and each has its own special attractions.

## Summer

The canal is vibrant in summer. Cicadas whirr constantly along its banks; sunflowers bloom along the higher reaches while grapes swell on the plains. The regions are alive with festivals and *ferias*; open-air concerts, plays, bull running and jousts are staged late into the hot nights. The smell of steaks or herrings on the barbeque fills the evening air.

The canal is busier: there are more boats along its length, queueing at locks and filling its harbours. The towpath has more cyclists but is never crowded or unpleasant, and it only takes a few minutes' cycling to regain a quiet part of the path. There is a great sense of camaraderie among cyclists along the path. You meet and re-meet people pedalling at your pace. Fellow cyclists exchange tips on the route or on the activities around the canal.

On the downside the summer temperatures are high, and it can be difficult to cycle in the intense midday heat. Temperatures can soar to 40°C, and even the nights remain hot. June and July bring out mosquitoes and midges, which can be an irritation after dusk.

Plan overnight stops more carefully in July and August. Even campsites can fill up – although owners rarely turn cyclists away – and advance booking is advised. Hotels in towns holding festivals fill up quickly,

## CYCLING THE CANAL DU MIDI

*Christmas on the canal*

and almost every bed is taken at weekends and bank holidays.

### Spring/Autumn
These are pleasant seasons for cycling the canal. Spring comes early in the Mediterranean area; from mid-February to June the days lengthen and warm, flowers bloom, butterflies emerge, swallows and martins return.

The area retains its warmth into late October. The shortening days are warm enough for shorts and T-shirts; the sea is still warm enough for swimming. It is an ideal time for cycling with daytime temperatures reaching the 20°C or more. Note, however, that nights are cooler, and the average rainfall is higher in May and June in the Toulouse to Carcassonne region than in earlier or later months.

Tourist numbers increase and decrease in spring and autumn respectively, and most tourist attractions are open. It is easy to find hotel rooms and seats in restaurants. The festival season starts in late spring and declines in autumn.

### Winter
Far fewer tourists cycle the track from November to January, although the leafless trees and bushes mean that visibility is improved. There are certain seasonal attractions such as Christmas markets and fairs, and theatres and concert halls also mark Christmas and the New Year with special productions.

Sunny days are less frequent; there will be very few biting insects, and none of the extreme heat you are likely to encounter in summer.

The difficulty with cycling in winter is that the days are shorter, colder and wetter. The canal can freeze during cold nights and there is always a danger of prolonged rain and sometimes even snow. Storms and flash floods are more likely, and winter storms can be violent.

Small hotels and *chambres d'hôtes* (bed and breakfasts) often close for winter, as do campsites. This may restrict your choice of accommodation but you should always be able to find something – with the exception of the days around Christmas.

### Different climatic zones

The weather varies from Toulouse to Sète; Toulouse has a temperate climate, changing to Mediterranean as the sea is approached. The weather is drier and warmer overall closer to the Mediterranean.

The area around Carcassonne and the hills and mountains north of the canal are prone to spectacular thunderstorms throughout the year. Heavy rain causes flash flooding and winter storms have wreaked havoc in certain years. Markers on the edge of the canal show the high water levels in the floods of 1953. On 12 November 1999 the Aude river burst its banks, killing over 30 people, uprooting trees, destroying vineyards and leaving large areas of land in the river basins submerged.

## HOW TO USE THIS GUIDE

This guide divides the canal into five stages:
- Toulouse to Port Lauragais
- Port Lauragais to Carcassonne
- Carcassonne to Homps
- Homps to Béziers
- Béziers to Sète.

Information is also given on short detours to sights close to the canal, and longer excursions into the surrounding countryside. The excursions are to:
- St-Férréol, the reservoir that feeds the canal
- Lastours, a former Cathar stronghold
- Minerve, a Cathar town set above the Cesse gorges
- Narbonne and Port la Nouvelle
- Vendres lagoon and the Aude river
- the Portiragnes marshes, home to flamingos and other wildlife.

Places meriting a short detour are also listed (detour lengths are not included). Each section of the canal, and the length of the excursions, are given in kilometres.

Fit cyclists could complete the main canal in two days – possibly even one – though they might put themselves and others at risk in attempting to do so, and little of the canal would be seen and enjoyed. This guide is written for those who want to explore the canal and visit the main attractions along the way. For

*Cycling the Canal du Midi*

example Carcassonne Cité, a UNESCO World Heritage Site, merits at least a half-day visit.

Those planning a week-long holiday should concentrate on the main canal and some of the short detours. Fitter cyclists may wish to include one of the excursions. Reasonably fit cyclists should be able to complete the canal and the excursions in two weeks. Those travelling the canal by boat, or living or holidaying in the region, will be able to use the guide to plan day or overnight trips.

The stage planning table in Appendix 1 will help you to plan days of the right length for you.

## HISTORY

### Early people

The countryside through which the Canal du Midi runs has a rich history, and has been inhabited and farmed since prehistoric times. Archaeological excavations in Valros, about 20km north of the canal at Vias, have revealed Neolithic burial pits, skeletons and artefacts from approximately 5000BC.

Seafaring cultures had easy access to the Languedoc across the Mediterranean Sea. Agde was originally an ancient Greek city; its ready supply of volcanic rock and rich

Celts and Romans shaped the region

volcanic soil for agriculture made it an attractive base for trade in the 7th century BC. Archaeological remains from that period can be seen in Agde's museum.

Evidence of the indigenous Ibero-Languedoc people can also be found close to the canal. The Oppidum d'Enserune is near Colombiers, about 2km from the tunnel at Malpas. This rocky hill was occupied continuously from 550BC in the Iron Age to the 1st century AD.

## Celts and Romans

The Celtic Volcae-Tectosages people spread throughout the southwest of France in the final three centuries BC, and ruled from Toulouse to Béziers. The latter was one of their principal towns and their name for the town – Baetarra (the house close to the ford) – eventually evolved into Béziers. The Volcae struck a treaty with the Romans at the end of the 2nd century BC when the latter established the province of Gallia Transalpina. The Volcae broke the treaty and captured the Roman garrison in Toulouse. The Romans retaliated, and subsequently the lands became part of their Gallic province.

The Romans established themselves quickly, leaving their mark across the entire region. They developed towns such as Narbonne, and Julius Caesar renamed Gallia Transalpina as Gallia Narbonensis. Unlike the other three provinces in Roman Gaul – Aquitania, west and south of the Loire, Celtica (or Lugdunensis), central France and Belgica in the north – Gallia Narbonensis had a civilian governor nominated by the Roman senate and was not a legionary garrison. The others were imperial provinces, with their governors appointed by the emperor and each with a legion.

The wine trade flourished during Roman times, and wine and other produce were exported to Italy. This trade presumably funded the extensive building and expansion of towns and cities. Towns such as Bram flourished and had a theatre and pottery works, and the Oppidum of Carcasa developed into the town of Carcassonne.

The Roman infrastructure is still in evidence today. The *Via Domitia* (Domitian's road) links Rome with the Iberian Peninsula. Part of it is visible in Narbonne, and a stretch can be walked at Pinet, a village 8km north of Marseillan at the Mediterranean end of the canal. Roman bridges and aqueducts can be found throughout the region.

The Roman Empire's decline had major ramifications for southwest France. In AD418 the Roman Emperor Honorius gave the Visigoths control of Gallia Aquitania in return for their help in regaining control of the Iberian Peninsula.

## Visigoths and Saracens

The Visigoths lost control of much of their Gaulish kingdom to the Franks following the battle of Vouille near

Poitiers in AD507. Little remains of the Visigoth kingdom with the exception of a few buckles, belts and bronzes, but the Visigoths live on in place names such as Alaric Mountain (south of the canal at Puicheric), named after their King Alaric.

The Languedoc was sandwiched between warring nations during the following centuries. The Saracens or Moors moved north in the 8th century and took Narbonne in AD720. In the following year a Frankish army defeated the Saracens in the Battle of Toulouse. They encircled the defeated troops and killed them, one of the worst military episodes in Muslim history.

Defeats at the hands of the Frankish leader, Charles Martel or Charles the Hammer, and King Pippin the Younger ended the Moors' permanent presence north of the Pyrenees in the Languedoc. The Moorish armies did cross the mountains in following centuries and in AD920 reached the gates of Toulouse, but failed to establish a permanent presence.

### Troubadours

This mix of religions, races and people may have contributed to the development of a more liberal and tolerant society in southwest France. At the beginning of the second millennium the region developed its own distinct code of nobility. The poetry of the troubadours from the 11th century exemplifies the sophisticated, artistic culture thriving there.

The troubadours composed songs and poetry in Occitan on the theme of courtly love. Their work was highly stylised and dealt with heroic feats, war, natural beauty, philosophy, honour, and love – passionate, unrequited and illicit.

This flourishing art angered the Roman Catholic Church. The verses often praised much that the Church opposed – especially physical love, adultery and romance. Satirical poems and songs about the Church and the clergy did little to assuage the former's anger. It is not surprising that the troubadours were seen as subversives when the Church began persecuting the Cathar faith.

### The Cathars and the Crusade

When driving towards southwest France motorway signs announce that you are entering the Cathar country. Memories of the atrocities committed 800 years ago are still fresh.

Catharism was a form of Christianity that evolved in the 10th century. Cathars could not reconcile the world's evil with a just and good God. They believed that evil must come from an evil God who controlled the material world, while the good God was responsible for the spiritual one. These beliefs were similar in part to those of the earlier Gnostics.

The Cathar church had a simple structure. The clergy were called Good Christians, *Bons Hommes* and *Bonnes Femmes* (good men and good

# HISTORY

*Cathar influence is still strong*

women). The believers were called the *credens*. The church had bishops, each supported by two deacons. The Cathars had one sacrament: the consolation. It served multiple purposes from initiation to ordination, confession and preparation for death. The Good Christians administered the consolation.

The Cathars prayed and fasted regularly. They shunned meat, eggs and diary foods; they ate fish, oil, vegetables and fruit. On fast days they took bread and water. The local population in southwest France admired the Cathars' piety and contrasted it with the lifestyle of the Roman Catholic clerics. The Cathars were perceived as practising what they preached.

The Roman Catholic Church became increasingly concerned about the growth in adherents of counter-religions, who were described as heretics. From the mid-11th century the popes condemned heresy in increasingly trenchant terms. In 1056 Pope Victor II excommunicated (expelled from the Church) heretics and their accomplices. The Church ordered the burning of heretics throughout the 12th century in towns across Europe.

Lotario Conti, a student of theology and canon law, was elected pope in AD1198. The 38-year-old chose the name Innocent III. He was greatly concerned about the spread of heresy – particularly in the Languedoc – and issued a decree legalising the seizure

19

*Cycling the Canal du Midi*

The crusade – a cruel and vindictive campaign

of heretics and property belonging to their supporters. He then put pressure on Raymond VI, Count of Toulouse, to act against the Cathars. Raymond VI was a vassal of Pedro II of Aragon, whose kingdom stretched across the Pyrenees from northern Iberia. Raymond was closely related to the Trencavel family who controlled Carcassonne.

In January 1208 Raymond VI met the pope's legate, Pierre of Castelnau, to persuade the latter to revoke an excommunication pronounced against him (Raymond VI had refused to support Pierre's campaign against the Cathars). The meeting between the two men was acrimonious. The following day some of Raymond's men attacked Pierre of Castelnau's party as they prepared to cross the Rhone, and killed the legate. Pope Innocent III used the murder as a pretext for declaring a crusade against Raymond and offered his lands as booty. The pope put his legate, Arnaud-Armaury, a former abbot, in charge.

A crusader army of 50,000 men reached the region in June 1209. They headed west from Valence (sparing Montpellier as a Roman Catholic city) and set up camp on 20 July in the abandoned town of Servian, near Béziers. Béziers refused to give up 210 named Cathars and prepared for a siege. On 22 July some young men came out of the town to jeer at the crusaders. They were chased by camp followers and failed to close the town's gate; the crusaders rushed inside and began sacking the town. The townspeople crowded into churches where priests celebrated mass. The crusaders, acting on Arnaud-Armaury's dictate to 'kill them all, God will know his own', slaughtered every man, woman and child; it is estimated that they butchered up to 20,000 people. At one stage they were reputed to be up to their knees in blood and gore.

The crusaders moved swiftly from Béziers and took Carcassonne. Simon de Monfort was appointed crusade leader and he picked off the towns in the surrounding countryside. His campaign was cruel and vindictive. For example in Bram, de Montfort – allegedly accompanied by Domingo de Guzman, later canonised as St Dominic – ordered his men to cut off the ears, noses and top lips of the defenders. He ordered that all but one should have their eyes gouged out and that the final defender should have one eye gouged. That person was forced to lead his blind companions from the town to seek sanctuary in Carabet at Lastours.

The crusade took the surrounding fortresses by siege, Minerve and Lastours among them. The crusaders' major victory came at Muret in September 1213 on the banks of the River Garonne. Poor generalship and the death of King Pedro II gave Simon de Montfort the day.

The campaign continued as the forces of the crusades tightened their hold on the lands in the south. The pope appointed the Dominican order as inquisitors to rout out the remaining heretics. The Cathars fled to isolated mountain forts – these falling one by one over the following century – until the last known Cathar was burnt at the stake in 1321.

**Wars and turmoil**
The region was caught up in the turmoil of the Hundred Years' War between England and France which began in 1337. It suffered famines in 1332 and 1374 and plague in 1348, when a third of the region's population died. English armies and mercenaries pillaged the area during a period of general lawlessness. The Hundred Years' War came to an end in 1453.

The War of Religion between Protestant and Roman Catholics had a major impact during the 16th century. Many of the towns and villages along what was to become the route of the Canal du Midi changed hands.

Despite a revolt by Henri II of Montmorency in 1632, the 17th century saw the French establishing greater regional control and the country emerging as a major power. However, France lost many of her colonies to England in the late 18th century, and relations between parliament and the aristocracy became increasingly bitter. The French Revolution in 1789 brought about the fall of the monarchy and the establishment of a republic in 1793.

Despite wars, including the Napoleonic Wars, the south of France continued to develop and prosper in the 18th and 19th centuries. The Canal du Midi, inaugurated in 1681, contributed greatly to this improvement. Wine production became a major source of wealth – the lifeblood of the region. In 1875 phylloxera attacked and destroyed the region's vine plants. The old varieties were replaced by American ones and the vineyards were re-established. However, the break in production allowed wine from French colonies in North Africa to gain a foothold in the French market.

In 1907 wine producers in the south of France revolted against declining prices. Specifically, they protested against the practices of traders who were watering down wine and adding sugar to boost strength and yield. Initially protests took place in the main towns. But these demonstrations gained momentum and threatened to lead to Occitan becoming a separate republic. The French government ordered the arrest of the revolt's leaders in June 1907. Crowds gathered in the major towns to prevent the arrests; in Narbonne, troops fired on the crowds and killed five people. These killings incensed the local population and they attacked and burned down public buildings in several towns. Troops in Agde mutinied and marched to support the protesters in Béziers.

The leader of the protests, Marcelin Albert, met the French prime minister Georges Clemenceau in Paris. The prime minister outwitted the wine producer and undermined his authority by saying that he had broken down in tears during the meeting. The government granted some minor concessions and the revolt died out.

The region played an important role in the two World Wars in the 20th century. A disproportionately large number of its men were lost in the trench wars in World War I. In World War II the Pyrenees became a stronghold for the French Resistance.

## THE CONSTRUCTION OF THE CANAL

Roman and French rulers long dreamed of linking the Atlantic and Mediterranean seas. It was the ingenuity and dogged persistence of one man, Pierre Paul Riquet, that made it reality.

There was a strong commercial reason for linking the two seas. The route around the coast of Spain was 3000km long, and the journey was perilous. Pirates preyed on cargo ships and winter storms destroyed them. Road transport was also difficult, and carts couldn't carry large volumes of goods. On top of these difficulties the authorities wanted a secure transport system that was within their control.

Pierre Paul Riquet was born in Béziers on 29 June in either 1608 or 1609. His father was a businessman and lawyer. Riquet became a tax collector and was responsible for raising taxes to provision the king's army in the region, amassing enormous personal wealth in the process.

While travelling the countryside on business, Riquet pondered on how to connect the Atlantic and the Mediterranean. The core problem was finding a reliable water supply to replenish any canal. In company with Pierre Campmas, Riquet evaluated possible water supplies in the Montagne Noire and worked out how a canal could be supplied. The king granted him permission to start work on the Canal du Midi in 1666. Riquet, who was neither an engineer nor architect, oversaw the works for the next 14 years. The canal was a major innovation and included significant innovations in its construction. For example, the dam on the lake in St-Férréol was the first of its type in Europe.

*Pierre Paul Riquet*

*Cycling the Canal du Midi*

*The plaque marking Pierre Paul Riquet's final resting place in St Étienne cathedral*

Riquet employed 12,000 men and women to dig the canal and put the 63 locks in place; they built bridges, aqueducts and lock-keepers' houses. They hacked out and blasted the tunnel at Malpas and created the ports in towns and villages along the way. The renowned French military engineer Marshal Sebastien le Prestre de Vauban oversaw some of the major works, such as the aqueduct over the Cesse river.

Riquet did not live to see the Canal du Midi in operation; he died in Toulouse in 1680, just seven months before it was opened. Riquet gambled his family's fortune funding the construction, but his sons recouped this when the canal began generating revenue.

*Port de Bassin de L'Embouchure (Stage 1)*

## CULTURE: FESTIVALS AND SPORT

The Languedoc has a rich culture and heritage, which can be experienced through the many festivals and celebrations which take place in the cities, towns and villages along the Canal du Midi. Continuous settlement, wars and industry have moulded both people and landscape.

Toulouse, Carcassonne and other large towns host international festivals, especially in summer. Carcassonne's festival runs for the month of July and includes concerts from international rock acts, the staging of operas, and a major fireworks display on Bastille Day, 14 July. Béziers hosts a *feria* in mid-August, which includes a bullfighting festival in its arena as well open-air concerts and performances.

There are smaller festivals in other towns and villages throughout the summer, and a wide variety of entertainment on offer: classical, jazz, rock and blues concerts; pageants and communal lunches. Southern villages organise bull-running through their streets. Wine festivals generally take place in autumn (although wine plays a significant part in most festivals).

Sports are important too. This is the heartland of French rugby – the cycle route passes close to the shell-shaped Mediterranean rugby stadium in Béziers. Toulouse is a great rugby centre, and the game dominates the city during major national and club fixtures.

## CYCLING THE CANAL DU MIDI

*Water jousting is a popular canal sport*

People play *petanque* all along the route, a form of bowls where players stand in a circle or behind a line and throw metal balls as close to a *cochonnet* or jack as is possible. The game is played on gravel or hard surfaces, and you'll have to cycle around games on parts of the towpath. Special floodlit areas in some towns and villages facilitate evening competitions.

One of the more unusual sports encountered on the canal is water jousting or *joutes nautiques*. Two teams in heavy rowing boats equipped with an elevated platform at the stern row towards each other. A jouster carrying a wooden lance and a shield stands on each platform; each uses his lance to try and push his opponent off his platform and into the canal. Sète is the major centre for *joutes*, but it is popular all along the canal.

# PRACTICALITIES

## GETTING THERE AND GETTING AROUND

### By air

There are four commercial airports close to the canal: Blagnac, Toulouse; Salvaza, Carcassonne; Béziers-Cap d'Agde; and Frejorgues, Montpellier. The airports at Toulouse, Carcassonne and Béziers-Cap d'Agde are less than 10km away. Montpellier's airport is approximately 40km from Sète.

Toulouse has flights to and from major European cities. Carcassonne is a base for low-cost airlines with flights from cities including London, Dublin and Brussels. Béziers-Cap d'Agde extended its runway in 2007 with the intention of attracting flights from major European centres. There are regular flights from Bristol and London. Montpellier has internal flights as well as flights from some international cities including London and Edinburgh.

Ryanair (www.ryanair.com) is the main airline serving southwest France from Ireland and the UK. It serves Carcassonne, Montpellier and Béziers-Cap d'Agde. British Airways (www.britishairways.com) and Aer Lingus (www.aerlingus.com) fly to Toulouse. Airlinair (www.airlinair.fr) and Air France (www.airfrance.com) fly to some or all of these airports, but not directly from the UK or Ireland.

Those changing planes in Paris should check where the connecting flight leaves from; it may be necessary to transfer to another airport.

Advise your airline that you plan to bring a bike when you book your flight. You'll be required to turn the pedals inwards or take them off entirely, and must also fix the handlebars sideways. You then have to pack the bike into a hard or soft holder, deflating the tyres to avoid their bursting under decompression. Airline charges for carrying bikes vary; expect to pay approximately €30 per flight.

Make sure that you book your flight well in advance. Airlines limit the number of bikes on each flight – some as few as six per plane.

### By car

The Canal du Midi is easily reached by road. You can drive to the south of France from most parts of Western Europe; the French motorway network will deliver you to the canal in 12 hours from most of its borders. Most motorways are tolled and these can be expensive. Websites such as www.mappy.fr enable you to plan your route and will also calculate your toll charges.

Autoroute 61 (A61) runs very close to the canal between Toulouse and Narbonne; it can also be reached

## Cycling the Canal du Midi

easily from the A9 between Narbonne and Sète. The A75 will end near the canal, close to Béziers, when the final section of that motorway is completed in 2010.

British car ferries sail to a range of French ports including Dieppe, Calais, Boulogne, Le Harve, Cherbourg, St Malo and Roscoff.

When it comes to leaving your car somewhere while cycling the Canal du Midi, there are long-stay car parks in towns and cities, and at railway stations. Hotels and guesthouses will often let you leave your car there for a day. There is often space to park close to the canal where roads cross it, or where it goes through smaller villages.

### By train

There are train stations at intervals along the length of the Canal du Midi in Toulouse, Castelnaudary, Bram, Carcassonne, Narbonne, Port la Nouvelle, Béziers, Agde and Sète. High speed trains – TGVs – link France's (and, increasingly, Europe's) major cities. These serve Toulouse, Carcassonne, Narbonne, Agde and Sète. Direct or indirect connections to all of these run from cities and towns in France. The Eurostar connects with the French high-speed service and runs services from three international stations: St Pancras in central London; Ebbsfleet, just off the M25 (junction 2); and Ashford in Kent.

The French railway company, Société Nationale Chemin de fer Francais (SNCF), allow bikes on their trains. Timetables can be checked on their website, www.voyages-sncf.com.

Bicycles must be prepared for carriage on the Eurostar services and certain TGV and Corail (intercity) French trains. The bike must fit into a cover measuring 120 x 90cm. Eurostar specifies that handlebars, saddle and wheels must be removed and placed separately into the cover. The bike can then be taken as hand baggage, together with the panniers. Alternatively, it may be placed in a baggage compartment free of charge.

Eurostar offers a registered baggage service, operating between London, Paris and Lille Eurostar terminals. They guarantee the bike will be available for collection within 24 hours of registration, and advise you to send your bike ahead so that it is there when you arrive. Eurostar charge £20 for this service. Within France, SNCF provide a similar door-to-door service (home or train station) for €49 (figures from 2008).

Some TGVs and Corails have special compartments for bikes, which do not have to be dismantled to use these. There is a €10 charge; make the reservation when booking your ticket. All the local (TER) trains allow you to put your bike in the baggage compartment. Some Corail trains also allow you to bring your bike on board. You may have to hang it by the wheel from a special hook on the carriage ceiling, so make sure that anything that might fall off has been removed.

## Getting there and getting around

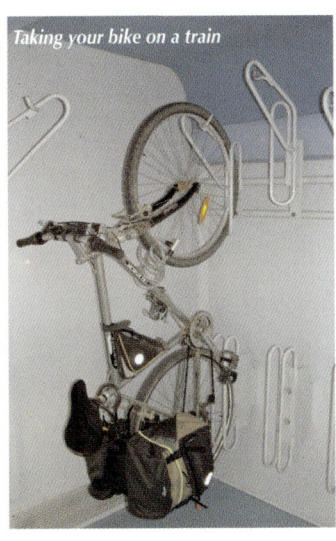
Taking your bike on a train

The SNCF website and timetables use a bicycle symbol to indicate trains with a bike compartment. There is a restriction on the number of bikes allowed on any train. Find out more on their website www.velo.sncf.com.

### Passports and travel requirements

Travellers from the UK and Ireland must have a valid passport to travel in France. Ensure that your passport remains in date for the length of your stay. France accepts identity cards from citizens of EU countries issuing these. As the UK and Ireland are not part of the Schengen agreement (which allows free travel without border controls between participating countries) a residency document or visa does not give you an automatic right to enter France.

The French embassy website (UK) www.ambafrance.ie gives information on who needs a Schengen visa.

Australian, Canadian, New Zealand and US citizens don't need a visa for a stay of less than 90 days, but require a full passport. Anyone (EU citizen or other) wishing to stay longer than three months must have a *carte de séjour*.

All visitors to France must have, ready for presentation at the border, documentary evidence of the reason for their visit, means of support for the duration, and their accommodation arrangements.

### Permit for parts of the towpath

The Voies Navigables de France (VNF) manages the Canal du Midi and controls the use of the towpath. It works with local authorities and where it is appropriate makes the path available to the public.

There are stretches of towpath that are not open to the public and a permit is needed to cycle on these stretches. I have yet to come across anyone checking for permits or preventing people from cycling on any section, but I carry one just in case.

You may apply for a permit by emailing us.adve.sn-toulouse@developpement-durable.gouv.fr giving the dates that you intend to travel, the number of people cycling and your intended route. The VNF accepts applications in English and responds quickly, but allow two weeks for processing.

## CYCLING THE CANAL DU MIDI

Bicycle bridge over the Orbiel (excursion to Lastours, Stage 3)

### Which bank?
We refer to riverbanks as being 'left' or 'right' depending on whether they are on the left or right of the direction in which the river water flows. Canal water, though, should flow as little as possible.

Technically, the canal water flows from Seuil de Naurouze – the highest point on the canal – to Toulouse in one direction and Sète in the other. Using the water flow to identify which bank to cycle causes confusion, so this guide refers to the northern and the southern bank. As you cycle from Toulouse to Sète, the northern bank is on the left and the southern on the right.

The points of the compass are used on the Narbonne canal system too. There, we refer to the eastern and western banks.

The route does at time change banks, and these changes are highlighted in sidebar text in this guide. Be sure to follow these even where the path appears to continue on the other side.

### YOUR BIKE

#### Arriving without one
It's possible to buy second-hand bikes relatively cheaply in the major towns along the Canal du Midi. Obviously, choice will depend on availability. Bikes may be in shorter supply in high season, pushing up the price and reducing choice.

Bikes are good value in France and you may decide to buy a new one there. Major chain stores such as

Decathlon (www.decathlon.fr) and Intersport (www.intersport.fr) in, or on the outskirts, of the major cities and towns, specialise in sports equipment. Remember, though, that even the large outlets may not have your size or the model that you want on the day you visit them. You'll find Decathlon and/or Intersport stores in Toulouse, Carcassonne, Narbonne, Béziers and Agde.

You can hire bikes in most centres along the canal. As mentioned, those renting out boats usually offer bike hire. These bikes vary in quality and deteriorate as the holiday season progresses. Hiring a bike is a good option if only planning to cycle for a day or two. However, the cost of bike hire has increased in recent years, and it may be cheaper to buy a second-hand bike than hire one for a prolonged period.

**Note:** Check which brake lever operates which brakes before you start to cycle.

### What type of bike?

You can match parts of the routes in this guide to any type of bike. I've used most sorts of bike on the towpath. The tarmac stretches from Toulouse to Port Lauragais and Béziers to Portiragnes are suitable for a racer or thin-wheeled training bike. These bikes may be used on the road excursions to St Ferréol and Minerve.

The bulk of the path is clay and bumpy. It can be cycled using a touring bike but an all-terrain bike (ATB) or hybrid is better. I prefer a bike with front suspension to absorb the constant bumps that might otherwise cause repetitive stress injury. A reasonable spread of gears is required if you make the excursions into the mountains. Good brakes are essential. Broader tyres (700 x 28) are better for dealing with rougher stretches. The path can become very muddy in wet weather and the heavy clay will collect on tyres with deep threads. Mud can clog brakes or immobilise wheels.

Consider bringing a bike with quick-release wheels, or fitting these if you haven't got them already. Assume that you will suffer at least one puncture on the route. Quick-release wheels make it a lot easier to swap a tube or fix a puncture.

A comfortable saddle is important. Gel-filled saddles or gel-filled covers absorb the harder knocks; a suspension saddle serves the same purpose.

Fit a water bottle holder to your bike frame. These are easy to attach and most bikes have nuts for attaching them. Ensure your water bottle fits snugly into the holder.

You'll need a rear carrier if you use panniers. This should be strong enough to take the weight of your bags and a tent if you plan to camp. Most carriers support a maximum load of 20kg.

A handlebar bag is very useful for holding valuables such as a camera, mobile phone and so on. Bags with a clear plastic map holder on top are handy.

Fix front and back reflectors on your bike. Reflectors on your spokes are worth fitting too as roads are crossed regularly along the canal. Bring front and rear lights; it's best to have detachable ones to avoid theft. However, the lights will be insufficient for cycling on the unlit stretches of the canal.

## Looking after your bike

Get your bike serviced before you leave. A basic repair kit is essential, and should include:

- puncture repair kit
- spanners and Allen keys to fit all nuts and bolts
- pump
- spoke tightener
- screwdriver matching the screws on your bike
- two replacement tubes
- replacement tyre
- replacement spokes and screws.

Learn how to change a tube and tyre before you set out. Get your local bike shop to show you how to adjust your brakes and gears. Find out which nuts you need to tighten regularly; for example, you should check the nuts on your carrier daily as these can work loose and shear.

There are bike repair shops in the main centres along the route (see Appendix 6). These repair bikes and sell the supplies that you may need.

## HEALTH AND SAFETY

France has an excellent health service. Most medium-sized villages have a health centre with a medical practice combined with paramedical services. Pharmacies (look for flashing green crosses) dispense medicines, and pharmacists give advice on basic illnesses or injury. French hospitals are clean and efficient.

Visitors from EU and EEA countries should carry an in-date European Health Insurance Card (EHIC) from their own health service. The card covers any medical treatment needed as a result of accident or injury. It applies to state provided services only, not to private; you will be treated in the same way as a state-insured person in France. The card also covers treatment for chronic or pre-existing illnesses. Find out more about the EHIC from the UK's Health Department website (www.dh.gov.uk). The cards can be applied for online in Ireland and the UK.

Visits to the doctor's clinic will cost between €20 and €25. The clinic hours are usually displayed on the door or wall together with the number of an out-of-hours service. French doctors still make home visits and may come to you if you are too unwell to reach the surgery. Hospitals and pharmacies also charge; the doctor and pharmacy is paid at the time of the visit, but hospitals will bill your home address for treatment received in France.

It is important that cyclists taking medication and/or suffering from

## HEALTH AND SAFETY

*Cycle lane marking*

long-term medical conditions should carry their medication and a description of their treatment at all times. They should make sure that they have the generic name of their medication and the dose in milligrams or millilitres. Those suffering from a long-term medical condition should wear an identity pendant and/or bracelet engraved with their medical details. The registered charity MedicAlert provides such material together with an emergency contact telephone service (www.medicalert.co.uk).

Contact the Service d'Aide Medicale Urgence (SAMU) in the event of a life-threatening illness or accident; their telephone number is 15. They may connect you to an English-speaking specialist or pass your call to a private ambulance service. Make sure that you have the precise address and location within that address (for example hotel room number and floor) when you call.

Private dentists provide most of the dental care in France.

### Insurance

All cyclists are advised to take out proper health and travel insurance. It is essential for those without the protection of the EHIC and advisable for those entitled to it. This should cover unlikely eventualities such as repatriation in the event of serious illness or accident, prolonged hospitalisation and the cost of major medical procedures.

## On the trip

Make sure that you never have to call upon your insurance policy. A few simple precautions should prevent most of the misfortunes that are likely to befall the canal path cyclist.

**Before you go** Cycling can be a vigorous exercise. One of the good points about cycling along the canal towpath is that you can do it at your own pace. Nevertheless, if you have not cycled or exercised for a long time, you should have a full physical check-up.

It's best to do some cycling at home before you head for the canal. A small amount of training will help you to avoid stiffness, aches and pulled muscles or tendons. The key is to build up gradually from short cycles, under half an hour, to longer, half-day cycles.

**On the track** The most important precaution you should take when cycling is to wear a helmet. Helmets reduce greatly the risk of serious head injury. A fall is a constant potential hazard on the towpath and a helmet gives some protection. There is a temptation to discard your helmet in hot weather –don't. Pour water over your head or stick it under a tap.

Wear brightly coloured highly visible jerseys. Roads are crossed regularly and cycled on occasionally. The road from Marseillan to Sète can be

*Plane trees shade most of the towpath*

busy in summer and has cars parked on both sides, so make yourself visible.

The French countryside is sparsely populated and thus poorly lit. Use front and rear lights from dusk onwards; if possible avoid cycling at night.

**Note:** Remember, you cycle on the right in France.

**Dealing with the heat** The south of France gets extremely hot in summer. It can top 40°C during the day, and on some nights the temperature remains over 30°C. The canal region begins heating up in April and can remain hot into October. Plane trees shade much of the canal but exposure to direct sunlight is frequent, and sometimes you can be unaware of how hot it has become.

Always carry water and drink copious amounts; a good rule of thumb is one litre per hour. I usually carry a bidon (small water bottle) in a container on the bike's frame, and further supplies in my panniers or a bag on the rear carrier. Drink before you feel thirsty, and supplement your salt intake if you perspire a lot.

**Avoiding burning** Sunburn is the other major health risk for cyclists. It only takes 30 minutes' direct sunshine to burn, and this can ruin the rest of your cycle. This guide includes a number of excursions, such as the one to Port la Nouvelle, where there is little shade. Plan these trips so that you can rest at midday – the hottest time.

Use lots of high factor suntan lotion. Put it on all exposed skin. Cream the tops of your arms underneath your sleeves and your thighs under the edge of your shorts as these areas can be exposed as you cycle. Pay attention to your ears and nose. Protect your scalp under your helmet if you are bald or thinning.

Keep a shirt on – preferably a cycling jersey – at all times.

**Bites and stings** The canal, its banks, surrounding marshes, rivers, streams and irrigation channels provide ideal conditions for mosquitoes and biting midges. These don't usually bother you while you are cycling but can when you are stationary. Mosquitoes are particularly active at dusk and during the night. Plug-in burners and burning coils give good protection in rooms. Remember to plug these in or light them in the evening so that they start working before the mosquitoes become active.

You should consider bringing an insect-repellent spray or cream if you are allergic to mosquito or midge bites. Wear long-sleeved tops and long-legged bottoms. Pay special attention to wrists, ankles, neck and head. Creams or sprays containing DEET give good protection to exposed adult skin.

Lotions such as Calamine can reduce itching if you are bitten. Anti-itching creams bring relief as do antihistamine creams; topical antisteroids can also help. Keep an eye on bites to make sure that they don't become infected, and use an antiseptic cream if there are any signs of infection.

Along the canal you'll meet wasps, hornets and bees in all seasons but winter. You can treat stings with over-the-counter creams or lotions. Watch out for an allergic reaction and seek immediate treatment. You should also attend the doctor if stung in or near the mouth or eyes.

**Larger pests** Regular cyclists know that dogs can be a hazard on any ride. French dog owners generally keep their pets under control, but the canal towpath is a favourite route for dog walkers so be careful.

There are a few poisonous snake species found in and around the canal, but most are harmless.

There are weaver fish (*vif*) in the Mediterranean. These burrow into the sand below the shallow waters at the sea's edge. The fin-spines stick into your feet, and should you be unlucky enough to stand on one the pain is excruciating and instantaneous. Put your foot in very hot water, as hot as you can tolerate, to denature the poison injected. Usually the lifeguards on the beach will help you (if on duty). The sting, though painful, is not fatal, but you should seek medical treatment in case other problems develop.

**Cuts and scratches** The edge of canal is lined with branches and briars and so you can expect to get the odd cut or scratch. Carry antiseptic cream, liquid or spray and treat these immediately.

**The canal water** There are rats living along the bank of the canal and swimming in its water. There is a risk therefore that the water may harbour Weil's or other diseases. The canal receives run-off and effluent from farms, and the water is undrinkable. Never swim in the canal, even though you may see local children doing so; it is forbidden and may put your health at risk. Wash yourself thoroughly should you get wet with canal water.

The water is a metre deep at the edges. Should an adult fall in he or she will be alright. The locks are potentially dangerous as they are deep, and you risk being held underneath the water by the currents should you fall in.

**Route hazards**

The canal carries hazards specific to cyclists. The plane trees along the banks are true friends for cyclists but occasionally they can be a problem. The trees shed small branches and twigs during windy weather. These are light and may catch in your wheels and brakes bringing you to a sudden surprise stop (I know – I broke my elbow in such a fall).

Some people who rent boats have little idea of how to work them. Be careful when approaching a boat that is mooring, or about to do so. I've been hit in the face twice by mooring ropes thrown by an inattentive crew

**HEALTH AND SAFETY**

*Common hazards to look out for on the towpath: mooring ropes and subsidence*

member, and have had to make a number of emergency stops when people have jumped in front of me from cruisers' decks. Watch out for carelessly thrown waste water.

Look out for mooring ropes stretched across the towpath and tied to trees or fences. At head height or body level these may cause an accident. Take care when approaching a boat moored away from marinas.

The canal company works constantly to maintain and repair the canal. The wash from boats and the burrowing of coypu, otters and rats undermines the bank. You will come across places where the bank has subsided. Stay well away from the water's edge as the bank may be eroded further and you may be cycling on an overhang.

People enjoy the canal in different ways. Youngsters (and the not so young) use stretches of it to learn how to rollerblade or cycle. Make sure to give other users plenty of room; use your bell to warn walkers and others of your approach. Remember to stick to the right – but don't assume that others will.

Down-and-outs and drunks sometimes sleep under bridges in major towns or camp out on the canal's verges. They are usually harmless, but it's best to avoid them in the evenings and at night. This problem is worst in Toulouse; avoid going under bridges there. The bridge west of Carcassonne is used in the same way.

**Keeping your bike and goods secure**

I've found the canal safe both personally and for my bike and goods. The people of the southwest of France are friendly and courteous. Police patrol towns and villages regularly, but even so take normal precautions against crime.

As regards personal safety, the usual rules apply. Toulouse, for example, is a cosmopolitan city and experiences the crime that goes with it. Avoid obvious dangers such as dark alleys and dingy pubs or clubs.

Avoid camping rough or bivouacking along the canal. An apparently quiet area may still be reached easily by road and leave you open to robbery.

Lock your bike any time you leave it unattended. Use stout locks for the front and the back wheels, and lock the bike to something solid and immovable. Secure quick-release saddles using wire loops you can buy for the purpose. It won't deter a determined thief but it will put off the opportunist.

Make sure that you carry your valuables with you and hidden; carry money, passport and credit cards separately. I usually put the most important items in a pouch strung around my neck and concealed under my jersey. I put money in a zipped pocket and credit cards in a wallet elsewhere on my person. Keep cameras and other valuables in a bag that you can detach easily and carry with you.

## ACCOMMODATION

There is a wide range of accommodation available along the canal, ranging from expensive hotels to very basic campsites. Your options include hotels, *chambres d'hôtes* (bed and breakfasts), *gîtes* (holiday homes for rent), camping and chalets in campsites.

Hotels vary from anonymous chains to small family-owned premises. The chain hotels are in major towns or close to the motorway, are relatively cheap and offer clean but basic rooms. You pay extra for breakfast and any other service. Chain hotels, such as B&B and Etap, are situated close to the canal in Toulouse.

The quality of smaller French hotels varies widely and you should check out rooms before you accept

Most hotels and *chambres d'hôtes* have lock-up garages or rooms where they will allow you store your bike during your stay. Some hotels let you take your bike into your room.

Insure yourself against theft, loss of or damage to your belongings. Check if your policy covers theft of your bicycle. Apart from your bicycle, money, cameras and other electronic equipment are the goods that thieves are most likely to target. Should you have the misfortune to lose your valuables, or be robbed, report this to the police and get a receipt. Insurance policies require you to keep your goods, money or travellers cheques safely; goods left unattended or unsecured are not covered.

*Chambres d'hôtes offer great value*

them. Cheaper hotels may have very limited facilities, and not all rooms are the same. You may find that the bathroom and toilet are shared by everyone on a corridor. Most rooms have a wash hand basin, while it is possible that you may be offered a room with a shower but without a toilet.

*Relais* hotels are a very French phenomenon. Truck drivers and commercial travellers are their main customers and they tailor their services for these clients. The rooms are functional. They offer good value particularly if you book dinner, bed and breakfast. Guests usually sit together at long tables to eat; wine is normally included in the price and bottles of red wine (usually) are distributed along the table, shared and refilled as required. The food is good and portions are large, although the menus are limited. *Relais* hotels are an excellent option if you are keen to meet and chat with French people.

Five-star hotels will charge in excess of €100 a night; chains charge between €60 and €80; smaller hotels may charge less than €60 a night. There may be a supplement for an additional person.

*Chambres d'hôtes* are the French equivalent of bed and breakfasts. Like small French hotels, they vary in price and quality. Usually, the quality is good and some are excellent, but a few are poor. Check the rooms in advance. Most *chambres d'hôtes* offer evening meals and these are usually communal. The standard of catering is usually very good and most use local produce. Charges vary greatly, with some charging up to €100 for a room a night, but most charge between €30 and €60 for bed and breakfast with evening meals costing an extra €12 to €20. Supplements for a second person apply.

*Gîtes* are usually booked in advance and for at least a week, and range from houses to apartments or wooden chalets. On occasions you may be able to hire one for an overnight or a few nights' stay. You cater for yourself – and provide your own towels and sheets – and they are usually well equipped.

Camping is a great option for canal cyclists, and there are campsites close to all the routes described in this guide. The sites vary from very basic, usually municipal, to five-star ones with swimming pools, restaurants, discothèques and tennis courts. Larger campsites may be noisy during the high season, and most are closed between October and April. Pitches for tents cost between €10 and €30 a night. Some campsites rent chalets or caravans by the night if they are available; these are normally rented by the week from Saturday to Saturday.

Note that all prices increase during the high season and accommodation becomes difficult to find. Hotels are open all year around in Toulouse, Villefranche de Lauragais, Castelnaudary, Bram, Carcassonne, Homps, Narbonne, Capestang, Béziers, Vias, Agde and Sète.

## EATING AND DRINKING

The Canal du Midi passes through land that produces an abundance of fresh food and wine. France is renowned for its cuisine and it finds its best expression in the Languedoc; restaurants and shops promote fresh local produce in season.

Farmers often sell their produce directly; you can buy fruit and vegetables for a very reasonable price. Asparagus comes into season in April, quickly followed by berries such as strawberries and raspberries. Vegetables also come into season early and you can buy new potatoes, courgettes, carrots and aubergines throughout the summer. Fresh, tasty tomatoes are available directly from producers along the route.

Figs are abundant in June and September, and can often be picked from trees growing close to the canal; melons grow in fields near the towpath. Autumn fruits such as cherries, apples and pears also grow close by. Almonds are produced in many places.

The presence of the canal boosted the wine trade in the 19th century. The trade continues, though it is declining in the face of competition from cheaper foreign wines. Local wines are excellent and can be bought directly from vineyards passed en route. It would be impossible to list all the wine-producing regions close to the canal but they include les Corbières, Minerve, Thau, Pinet, La Clape, Fitou and St Chinian. Popular varieties of grape are (reds) Grenache, Caringnan and Cabernet Sauvignon; (whites) Sauvignon Blanc, Viognier and Muscat Sec. Sweet Muscat is a popular fortified dessert wine.

The Mediterranean Sea is a great source of fish and seafood and Thau oysters can be bought from small outlets in villages close to the sea. There are fishmongers in the small towns and villages along the route too.

Meat is an important part of the French diet, and there are butchers' shops in all towns and many larger villages. Horse meat is still eaten in France and you may see signs for *viande cheval* or *chevaline*.

### Restaurants and cafés

There are relatively cheap restaurants and cafés along the canal, and those catering for tourists are only open

*The region is renowned for its range of excellent wines*

## Cycling the Canal du Midi

*Markets are a blaze of colour*

from after Easter to October. There is a wide range of eating opportunities from pizza outlets to traditional places with starched white tablecloths and formally dressed waiters.

Set meals are the cheapest option in most restaurants and lunches are usually the best value. A set lunch can cost as little as €11 a head and will include a starter, main course and dessert. In some cases, a quarter litre of house wine is included.

Meat and fish dishes are the main specialities. From Toulouse to Castelnaudary restaurants serve *cassoulet*, which includes pork, local sausages, haricot beans and garlic. *La teille Sètoise* is a pie with an octopus, onion and tomato filling seasoned with herbs and topped with pastry, brought to Sète by Italian fishermen in the late 19th century. Ratatouille is popular in the south of France and is best served at room temperature in summer.

Vegetarians are rarely able to benefit from set meals as the main course is usually fish or meat. French restaurants may attempt to serve vegetarians fish or chicken dishes, and some apparently vegetarian dishes, such as stuffed vegetables, may contain meat. You will find a wide range of salads, including warm goat's cheese salad, as alternatives. There are a few restaurants along the canal that specialise in tarts and quiches and there is always at least one vegetarian option. One of the best of these is at Castanet lock.

Restaurant closing times are strictly observed. You will find it hard to get lunch after 2.30pm and last orders for dinner aren't usually accepted after 9.30pm.

## Shops and markets

Shopping for food along the canal is a delight, in hypermarkets, supermarkets, small local stores, specialist shops, or from travelling vans and local producers. In addition there are markets, at least weekly, in most towns and large villages.

The boulangerie and patisserie form the cornerstones of village life, and villagers buy their bread and croissants fresh daily. Baguettes are excellent for picnics but will only stay fresh for a few hours.

Smaller shops open early in the morning at 7.30am and close between 12.30pm and 4pm in the afternoon. They close in the evening around 6.30 or 7pm. Some may open on Sunday morning.

French markets are a blaze of colour and scents, with stallholders selling everything from fruit and vegetable to clothes and hardware. The markets normally start at 8am and finish at 12pm. There are some evening markets in summer, often as part of festivals. Markets are usually held in the main square or along the main street. Larger towns such as Béziers and Narbonne also have covered permanent enclosed food markets open in the morning only.

# CYCLING THE CANAL DU MIDI

*Shopping is a delight*

## PACKING

**What to pack**

Those preparing for a cycle tour should follow the golden rule of packing: lay out everything you want to take and leave half behind.

Obviously the season will determine what clothes you take. Prepare for cold wet weather in winter; thermal undershirts and socks are worthwhile; cycling gloves are essential. Warm cycling jackets and long cycling trousers are also necessary, as are lightweight breathable waterproof tops and leggings.

Light cool clothes will be required in summer, but bring compact waterproofs in case of poor weather. Expect it to be hot. Light cycling tops and shorts are essential; these should be easy to wash and dry as they'll become very dusty quickly. Shorts should cover your thighs even on the upstroke when pedalling to avoid the risk of sunburn. Cycling shorts with a chamois leather pad are very useful; wash these daily to avoid saddle sores.

Sunglasses are useful throughout the year, but essential in summer. Buy pairs with removable lenses and replace the darkened glass with low-light glass in the evening. These are useful as protection against insects and dust. Bring a sunhat for those times when you are not cycling and not wearing your helmet. You'll need anti-sun lotions; anti-mosquito creams and lotions for treating bites; a small first aid kit with bandages, scissors, tweezers (for thorns or splinters) and antiseptic cream; a supply of any medication that you take regularly.

### What bags to use

A handlebar bag is well worth bringing. Use panniers to carry your personal effects; avoid taking a rucksack if you plan to cycle for several days as it can chafe shoulders and back.

Rear panniers will hold most of your possessions, and are available in a range of sizes. You can buy high-quality back panniers that are waterproof and easy to secure. Saddlebag-style panniers (three bags joined together) are another alternative; one bag sits on the pannier and the other two hang on either side.

Make sure that the bags don't impede your pedalling. Use panniers you can adjust to allow your foot free movement. The route is dusty, and some cyclists use plastic covers to protect their panniers.

Those wanting to carry a lot of gear should consider a bike trailer. These hold more but are harder to manoeuvre.

### Maps

The Institut Geographique National (IGN) produces the best maps for the route. Use the 1:100,000 maps known as *Carte de Promenade*. Three of these, numbers 64, 65 and 72, cover all the routes in this guide, and

*Bicycles are available for hire*

## MONEY, PHONES AND EMAIL

France's currency is the Euro; one Euro equals 100 cents. Money can be withdrawn using an ATM card from French ATM machines. Banks and hotels will exchange dollars, sterling and other widely-used currencies.

European bill-pay mobiles should work in France. Check with your provider if you are from outside the EU or using a pay-as-you-go phone.

Internet cafés offer internet telephone services too. Public phones will be found in most villages and towns and you will need a special telephone card, on sale in newsagents, to use these.

There are internet cafés in the larger towns, and France Telecom offers internet services in its main offices. Some hotels have WiFi available.

### Emergency numbers

Use the following numbers in the event of an emergency:

| | |
|---|---|
| Medical/SAMU | 15 |
| Police/Gendarmerie | 17 |
| Fire/Pompier | 18 |
| European emergency number | 112 |

The pan-European number (112) works in any EU country from any phone. Use this if you are using a mobile.

*St Sernin's basilica (Stage 1)*

# STAGE 1
## *Toulouse to Port Lauragais*

| | |
|---|---|
| **Distance** | 52km excluding detours |
| **Path** | Tarmac: nearly all dedicated cycle track |
| **Shade** | Very good to good |
| **Climb** | 50m |
| **Map** | 64 IGN *Carte de Promenade* |
| **Detours** | To Castanet-Tolosan, Montesquieu-Lauragais, Villefranche-de-Lauragais and Avignonet Lauragais |

Stage 1 starts in the beautiful city of Toulouse. The route follows cycle paths along the canal, passing through the city's hustle and bustle then leaving the suburbs behind and reaching the countryside. Cycle through a plain bright with sunflowers in summer, passing small towns and villages on route. The bell walls of the churches along the way are eye-catching and typical of the region. Most of the bridges, lock-keeper's cottages, locks and works were built at the same time as the canal. The route ends at the point where the canal receives the water that supplies and replenishes the system – the highest point. A monument commemorates the creator of the Canal du Midi, Pierre Paul Riquet, at the end of this stage.

**Toulouse**
Toulouse is called the 'Rose City' because of the red brick used in its main buildings. It's a bustling, lively place: the streets and squares buzz with conversation, markets and buskers. Steeped in history, the city is now a major centre for hi-tech industries such as space and aeronautics, and is home to the headquarters, production and research facilities of the European Airbus.

The River Garonne flows through Toulouse, linking it to Bordeaux and then the Atlantic. Merchants transported goods from the Atlantic along the Garonne until the Canal Latéral linking Toulouse and Bordeaux opened in 1856. Transporting goods on the river was difficult, and could be treacherous when it was flooded. The

## CYCLING THE CANAL DU MIDI

*The Garonne river flows through the city centre*

Canal Latéral completed Riquet's dream of linking the two seas with a reliable waterway.

Toulouse is a cycling city, and has a large network of cycle lanes, tracks, parking and bike hire. There are cycle tracks beside the Garonne river, canals and roads; cycle lanes shared with buses; and lanes that go against the flow of car traffic. The local authority produces a map of the cycle routes for Toulouse and its surrounding region, *carte des intinéraires cyclables*, available from the tourist office or the information office in Blagnac airport.

There are 2400 cycles available for hire from 253 stations within the city. A special card or account is needed to use these, or else a credit card issued by a French bank. A better option for those who want to hire a bike for a short period is a cycle hire service located beside the tourist office in the Donjon behind the Capitole.

Toulouse has an excellent public transport system including a metro and bus network with daily and weekly tickets available, and can be reached by train or plane. The main train station is **Gare Matabiau** on the banks of the Canal du Midi on Boulevard Pierre Sémard.

There are plenty of restaurants and cafés to suit most budgets; there are music bars and discos as you'd expect in a city with a large student population. Toulouse is a rugby town with both codes, union and league, represented. Festivals are held throughout the year, including Summer Toulouse, the Rio Loco, Piano aux Jabobins, Toulouse les Orgues and many more.

It's well worth spending at least one day sightseeing. The city boasts beautiful houses dating from the 15th to 17th centuries – the golden age, when merchants garnered considerable wealth from the production of the blue dye pastel (also known as woad, and produced from the leaves of the pastel plant). The city's narrow streets and squares make it a pleasant place to explore by bike or on foot. Note that street names are often in both French and Occitan. The River Garonne is lined with walks, parks and public spaces, and south-facing cafés close to the river on the right bank enable you to sit outside even in winter. The river can be viewed from any of a number of bridges, but the **Pont Neuf** offers the traditional view (and one of the best).

**Place du Capitole** is the city's central square, a large, impressive space dating from the 18th century. The main

*Place du Capitole is Toulouse's lively central square*

building is the city hall or Capitole, named after the capitouls or consuls (rich merchant rulers). Its 128m-long façade has eight columns representing the eight capitouls. Cafés and restaurants under arches around the square are great places to sit and watch the Toulousains go by. The Saturday and Tuesday morning markets concentrate on organic or local products; for much of the time the square is a stage for performers and musicians.

The tourist office is located in the **Donjon**, a 16th-century building restored by Villet-le-Duc in the 19th century, and can be reached through the central archway in the Capitole. As you pass through this archway note a plaque on the ground marking the spot where Henri de Montmorency was executed after his forces were defeated by the king's army at Castelnaudary. Cardinal Richelieu accompanied King Louis XIII to Toulouse to supervise the execution.

Three of Toulouse's many churches stand out as worth visiting. **Basilique St Sernin** was built on the site of an earlier basilica housing the remains of St Sernin. Sernin, bishop of Toulouse, was martyred in AD250 for refusing to take part in the sacrifice of a bull; he was tied to its legs and dragged down a flight of stone steps. The church, 115m long, was a major stopping point for large numbers of medieval pilgrims going to Santiago de Compostela in Spain. Key points to note are its multi-tiered bell tower, its beautiful doors and extraordinary interior.

Those interested in the Cathar religion and its persecution may wish to visit the church known as the Jacobins, the site of the first Dominican monastery founded in AD1216. The Dominicans are known as the Order of Preachers. Their founder, St Dominic, preached against heresy and the order later spearheaded the inquisition against the Cathar faith.

The church takes its name from the order's first church in Paris, St Jacques, and the monks consequently became known as the Jacobins. The order built the church, the monastery and the first university in Toulouse. The church is built in red brick and is a masterpiece of that era. The interior is divided into two naves, its relative narrowness and height adding to its impact; the sarcophagus of St Thomas Aquinas is given a central location. There is a charge to visit the cloisters.

**St Étienne cathedral** is of special interest to those cycling the Canal du Midi as it is the final resting place of the canal's creator and builder, Pierre Paul Riquet, buried close to a pillar on the right as you enter.

*The Jacobins cloisters*

The main part of the cathedral was built in the 13th century and contains an impressive choir with wooden stalls. One of the early stained glass windows dates from the 15th century and shows King Charles VII of France together with the Dauphin Louis, later to become Louis XI; there are also locally produced tapestries from the 16th and 17th centuries.

Toulouse offers many other attractions, including museums such as The Augustines (21 Rue de Metz) housing a collection that includes early Christian artefacts as well as sculptures and art from later periods. The St Raymond museum of antiquities (Place St Sernin) has displays of art and archaeology from early centuries to the middle ages. Specialist museums include the natural history museum (35 Allées Jules Guesde); the museum of the history of medicine (Hôtel Dieu St-Jacques, 2 Rue Viguerie – Pont Neuf); and Space City BP 25855, Avenue J Gonord. Les Abattoirs houses the museum of modern and contemporary art (76 Allées Charles de Fitte).

### *The canal in Toulouse*
The Canal du Midi begins in Toulouse at Des Ponts Jumeaux, three bridges in the Port de Bassin de L'Embouchure. The bridges cross the three canals: du Midi, Latéral and Brienne. The Canal de Brienne links the Garonne river to the port.

The port is reached by car by leaving the A620 at the Echangeur Des Ponts Jumeaux. There is parking close by in the Place d'Armes. Those arriving by train should leave the station onto Boulevard Pierre Sémard, cross the road to the canal and join the cycle path, taking a right to reach the Port de Bassin L'Embouchure. You will return by the same path.

In the port, the Canal Lateral is on the left, the Canal du Midi is in the centre and the Brienne on the right as you face the three bridges. Note a white marble bas-relief fixed to the Ponts-Jumeaux between the Canal du Midi and the canal de Brienne. Created in 1774, this commemorates the linking of the Mediterranean and the Atlantic through the construction of the Canal du Midi.

## STAGE 1 – TOULOUSE TO PORT LAURAGAIS

There is an old working water pump on the southern bank of the port, and on the opposite side a small park, suitable for picnics.

### Leaving Toulouse

Make certain that you follow the correct canal at Des Ponts Jumeaux. You need to begin on the northern bank of the Canal du Midi between the canal and the

map continues on page 55

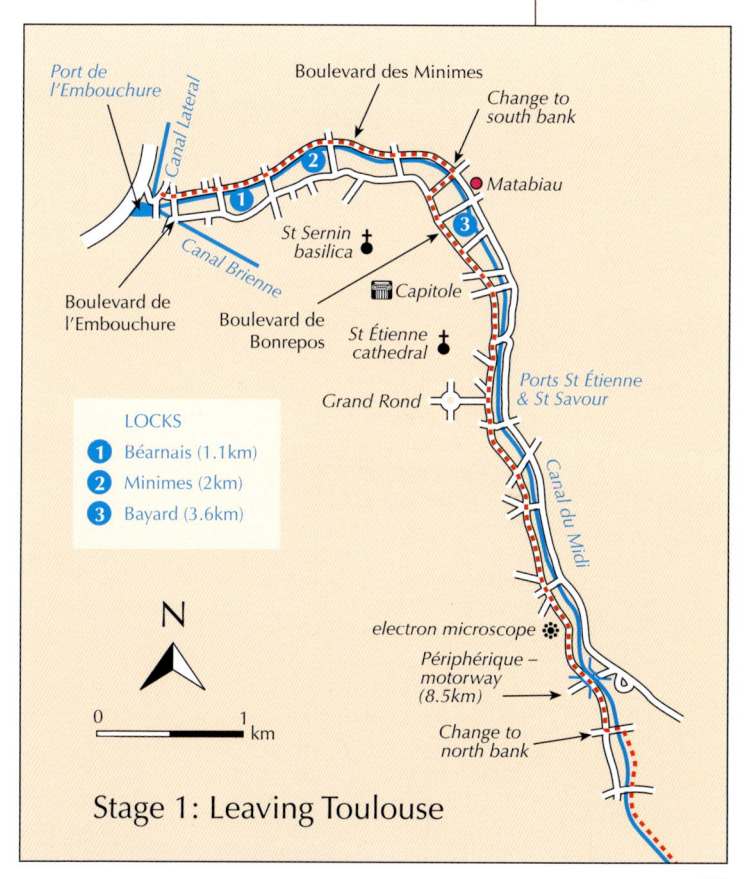

### Stage 1: Leaving Toulouse

**LOCKS**
1. Béarnais (1.1km)
2. Minimes (2km)
3. Bayard (3.6km)

Key locations shown on map:
- Port de l'Embouchure
- Canal Latéral
- Boulevard des Minimes
- Change to south bank
- Matabiau
- Canal Brienne
- St Sernin basilica
- Boulevard de l'Embouchure
- Boulevard de Bonrepos
- Capitole
- St Étienne cathedral
- Grand Rond
- Ports St Étienne & St Savour
- Canal du Midi
- electron microscope
- Périphérique – motorway (8.5km)
- Change to north bank

**Boulevard de l'Embouchure** on a dedicated cycle/pedestrian path. Reach this by climbing a short, 20m, path and crossing a small road (with a good view of the bas-relief to the right). Then take a broken tarmac track, pass under a bridge and join a proper tarmac surface.

Pass **Béarnais lock** after just over 1km. Go around and under footbridges and reach the second lock, **Minimes**, at 2km. After 2.7km, at the end of Boulevard des Minimes, take a bridge to the **south bank of the canal** and cycle on the track beside Boulevard de Bonrepos. ◄

> Cross to the south bank.

At 3.3km note the train station, **Matabiau**, on the northern bank of the canal. Reach **Bayard lock** at 3.6km with a plaque on the wall opposite giving the distances to the previous and next locks: 1668m to Minimes and 1222m to Castanet.

The towpath passes under a number of bridges, which are home to vagrants; stay on the path alongside Boulevards Riquet and Monplaisir. Note the first statue of Pierre Paul Riquet on your right. The path rises above, goes level with and drops below the canal level for 1km. There is a small park at 5.8km.

At 6km and three bridges after the Bayard lock reach **Ports St Étienne et St Savour**. St Etienne cathedral is south of the canal at this point. There is a bicycle hire (location), sale and repair shop (Movimento), and restaurants on barges moored nearby. Follow the path around a park and shortly afterwards cross a small wooden bridge. Take the left path and pass under a bridge beside the canal.

You are now in suburban Toulouse. At 7.7km pass a dome on your right, the site of the first electron microscope in Europe and no longer in use. At this stage the path runs alongside the towpath. Joggers and dog walkers use the towpath so it's best to stick to the cycle path.

The canal passes above Toulouse's *périphérique* road at 8.5km.

> Cross to the north bank.

At approximately 9km cross the canal by bridge and **cycle on the northern bank**. ◄ There are benches and very good shade. Pass a Formule 1 hotel on your left.

*Stage 1 – Toulouse to Port Lauragais*

## Stage 1: Outer Toulouse to Port Lauragais

- electron microscope
- Périphérique – motorway (8.5km)
- Change to north bank
- Ramonville St-Agne port
- Port Sud
- Castanet-Tolosan
- Donneville
- Montgiscard
- Ayguesvives
- motorway service area

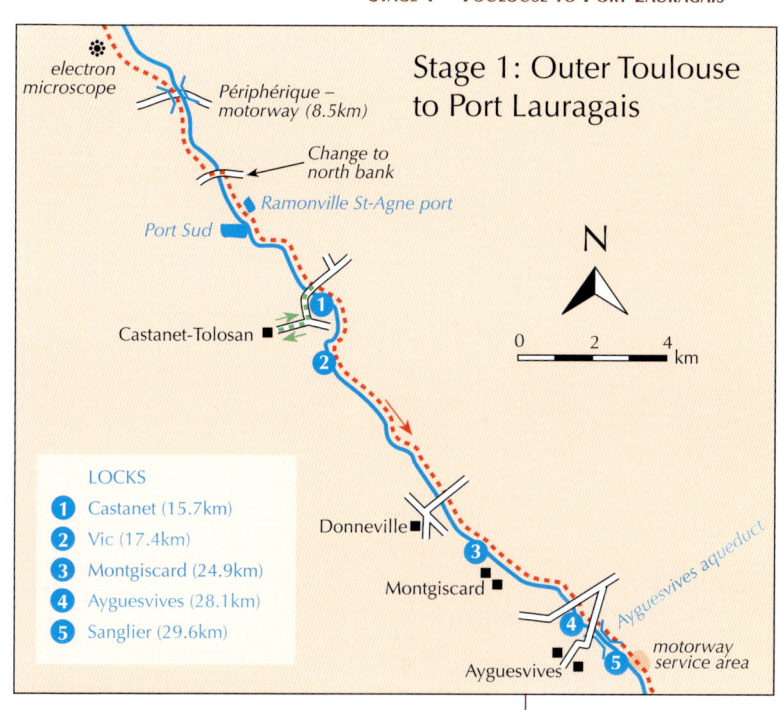

**LOCKS**
1. Castanet (15.7km)
2. Vic (17.4km)
3. Montgiscard (24.9km)
4. Ayguesvives (28.1km)
5. Sanglier (29.6km)

Ayguesvives aqueduct

map continues on page 58

*Sandwich bar in a disused submarine at Ramonville St-Agne port*

At approximately 12km arrive at the port of **Ramonville St-Agne**, where there is a nautical-themed restaurant and sandwich bar, the latter housed in an old submarine. Cross the port entrance by a bridge with a corkscrew descent. The affluent south port is on the other bank, approximately 1km later, and may be accessed via the bridge, Pont Mange Pommes.

The canal twists towards the bridge and lock at **Castanet-Tolosan**; there is a water point and toilets before the bridge. The café/restaurant at the lock is a good stopping point and popular at lunchtime.

> **Castanet-Tolosan** is approximately 4km from the canal on the south side and a good place to stock up on food and supplies. Reach the town through a series of small roundabouts, passing close to a large supermarket where you can stock up on basic provisions. Continue to the town on a cycle path.
>
> The town of Castanet has had a turbulent history. A fort in the town was sacked three times: by the Vandals (AD409), the Arabs (640) and the Black Prince in 1355. Cardinal Richelieu finally demolished it in 1626. Wellington's army used the village as a base in 1814. Few historic buildings remain today save for the old hospital (Le Vieil Hôpital) dating from the 13th century, and now used for social services.

From **Castanet lock**, continue on the north side of the canal towards **Vic lock** 1.7km away. Climb up from the canal and cross the road at this lock.

The canal continues to snake through the surrounding countryside from De Vic lock to **Montgiscard lock** 7.5km away. Pass close to the A61 motorway. In summer fields of sunflowers and large expanses of cereals grow near to the canal, which passes close to **Donneville** and the impressive bell tower of the church of St-Pierre. Riquet was the original builder of the old bridges here.

## Stage 1 – Toulouse to Port Lauragais

*Sunflowers near Montgiscard*

**Montgiscard** has a small port or broadening of the canal after the lock. A bridge leads to the town on the south bank where you'll find some shops. Note also a well-preserved *lavoir* on the southern bank, a public laundry using the canal water to wash clothes. There is a barge restaurant moored on the northern bank.

The path passes the **Ayguesvives lock** flanked by a brick mill built at the time of the canal's construction. Shortly afterwards cross the **Aqueduct d'Ayguesvives**. Constructed in 1687, it carries the canal over a river. The well-crafted brickworks jut into the canal.

Within 1.5 km reach **Sanglier lock**; the lock-keeper's house dates from 1752. After the lock find a small gate that leads into the motorway service area. You are not allowed to cycle in the service area, but you can walk through and use the drinking water taps and toilets.

*Cycling the Canal du Midi*

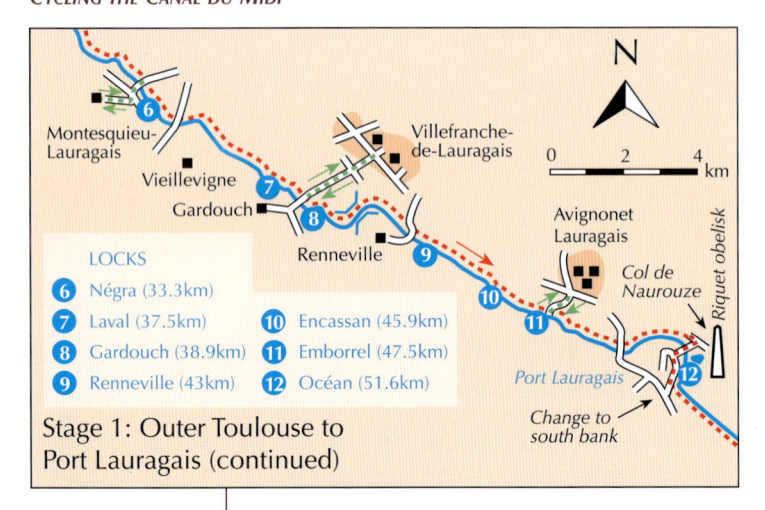

**Stage 1: Outer Toulouse to Port Lauragais (continued)**

LOCKS
- 6 Négra (33.3km)
- 7 Laval (37.5km)
- 8 Gardouch (38.9km)
- 9 Renneville (43km)
- 10 Encassan (45.9km)
- 11 Emborrel (47.5km)
- 12 Océan (51.6km)

map continued from page 55

**Négra lock** is nearly 4km further along the canal, and was a significant stopping point for barges. A small chapel named the Chapelle du Canal was built for travellers who stopped and dined at the lock.

### DETOUR TO MONTESQUIEU-LAURAGAIS

The small hilltop town of **Montesquieu-Lauragais** is a little over 1km from Negra lock and approximately 80m above the canal. To reach it, cross the bridge to the south side and follow the road (D11) (crossing the D16 after 200m) and climbing towards the village. Follow the road as it swings left and climbs to the town centre. The church and surrounding buildings dominate the skyline.

There are records of the town's existence from AD1271, and it is an excellent example of Toulousain architecture. The church of St Jacques was restored in the 18th century but retains its 14th-century bell gable. The town has two chateaux, one the town hall; the other can be glimpsed behind iron gates. This is a town to cycle through and experience its narrow streets, market building, houses and views of the plain and canal.

Return to the canal by the same route, making sure to pause and take in the views as you descend.

## STAGE 1 – TOULOUSE TO PORT LAURAGAIS

*Gate in Montesquieu-Lauragais*

Continue on the north bank of the canal. The path passes under the Tarbes–Foix motorway. The double **Laval lock** is 4.2km from Negra, and raises/lowers barges by 5.5m. Continue for a further 1.5km to **Gardouch lock**;

*CYCLING THE CANAL DU MIDI*

about 10m after the lock is a small *halt sanitaire* with water and toilets. After 1km cross the **Aqueduct l'Hers**; note the church tower of **Villefranche-de-Lauragais** on the left. The cycle track bypasses a farm house. A gate gives access to another motorway service area with water, toilets and picnic tables. Continue to **Renneville lock**.

### DETOUR TO VILLEFRANCHE-DE-LAURAGAIS

**Villefranche-de-Lauragais** is reached by a small road from Renneville lock approximately 2km away. Take the small road north from the lock, passing over the motorway. Follow the road as it curves left and runs alongside a railway track. The road crosses the tracks and you enter the town, passing a toilet block on the right. There is a *relais* hotel close by.

Villefranche-de-Lauragais is a lovely Toulousain town, with many excellent examples of redbrick buildings, three hotels, restaurants and a range of shops. The town is on the Via Aquitania (an old Roman road) and was founded in AD1270. As with other towns in the region, it suffered the ravages of war and reaped the benefits of peace. There are many fine houses and shop fronts, even if their glory has faded somewhat.

*Mermaid carved on the church door in Villefranche-de-Lauragais*

The church is the central building, and a notice beside the door states that Jeanne, Countess of Toulouse, and her husband Alphonse Poitiers, brother of St Louis, built the church in 1271. Another notice describes the bell tower as a 13th-century structure. The bell wall is striking, with two tiers of three bells supported between two pillars. There is an unusual clock below the bells and a mermaid carved on the main church door. The tower and church can be viewed easily from an open area across the road, and there is a 19th-century market nearby.

Take the same route back to the canal.

*Stage 1 – Toulouse to Port Lauragais*

Continue to **Encassan lock** 2.8km from Renneville. You will see a windfarm and the town of Avignonet Lauragais on the left. Continue to **Emborrel lock**.

*Faded glory in Villefranche-de-Lauragais*

*CYCLING THE CANAL DU MIDI*

## DETOUR TO AVIGNONET-LAURAGAIS

To reach Avignonet, leave the canal at Emborrel lock, heading north on the small tarmac road which crosses the motorway and continues towards the town. Turn right at a T-junction onto the N113 (a busy road). Take an immediate left turn, climbing into the town, and another left turn onto Rue du Pilori. There are public toilets on the way. A small sentry-post-styled building, the Poids Public, marks the entrance to the town.

This well-preserved historic town is worth visiting, and was the site of one of the key events in the war against the Cathars. On 28 May 1242, three Occitan knights and 12 of their sergeants broke into the quarters of the most hated inquisitors, Guillaume Arnaut and Étienne of St Thibéry. The assassins used axes to break into the room where the inquisitors slept and, using the same weapons, butchered the two together with nine of their supporters, including two Dominicans and a Franciscan. ▶

*Notre Dame-des-miracles church in Avignonet*

## STAGE 1 – TOULOUSE TO PORT LAURAGAIS

◀ The killings had a significant impact on the progress of the crusade, precipitating the siege and eventual fall of Montségur, the last major Cathar stronghold. The slain entered folklore by allegedly going to their death singing the Te Deum, and the event contributed to the elevation of Dominic, founder of the Dominican order, to sainthood. It is said that a local man kicked and laughed at the bodies of the dead priests, and subsequently suffered an incurable leg wound. This was attributed to the supernatural intervention of Dominic and adjudged miraculous proof of his saintliness.

The church of Notre Dame-des-miracles stands in Place d'Eglise in the town's centre, and was built between the 14th and 16th centuries on the site of a more ancient church. Its polygonal bell tower is over 40m high and dominates the surrounding Lauragais Plain; the nave is also 40m long, with seven chapels. The church is named after a statue found on the site of the original church, and has a plaque commemorating the murdered inquisitors.

The town has a number of other attractions. Mansions from the 16th century belonged to merchants who gained their wealth through the production of pastel made from the leaves of the pastel plant (woad). This gave an exceptionally deep blue, used for colouring paints and dyes, and this industry funded the development of Toulouse and the towns around the Lauragais Plain. There is an old market building on the main street, a stone tower and statue of a crusader (water tap beside it), together with a statue of Joan d'Arc.

Take the same route back to the canal.

From **Emborrel lock** continue on the northern bank of the canal. After 2km approach **Port Lauragais** and the Seuil de Naurouze. The main part of the port is a now a motorway service area with hotel, restaurants and shops, and an exhibition celebrating the history of the canal. A barge moored in the port within the service area offers bed and breakfast.

Should you wish to enter the service area, you can do so from the southern side of the canal. Cross the canal using a bridge situated at approximately the point where the port buildings come into view (2km after Emborrel lock). Turn left after crossing and follow the sign for Port Lauragais. Enter the service area (*aire*) through a car park on your left.

Return to the bridge to rejoin the canal. Follow the path as it curves north just opposite the Port Lauragais restaurant. Now leave the tarmac path and continue on a gravelly surface. Pass under a railway and later a road bridge before coming to a small bridge. You have now reached the public park around Port Lauragais.

---

Carry straight on to visit the Riquet obelisk built to commemorate Pierre Paul Riquet. The way is marked with small blue signs. Follow the plane-tree-lined avenue; turn left at a small bridge and then right after an information centre. The path to the 20m-high obelisk is 200m on the left, just before the Moulin (mill) de Naurouze. Built in 1827, the obelisk carries a bas-relief of the Riquet coat of arms and representations of the gods Minerve for wisdom and Mercury for commerce. Nymphs represent the Montagne Noire watering the plain; old Neptune faces the ocean while Venus faces the Mediterranean.

The **Col de Naurouze** at 189.43m is the highest point on the canal. The water that replenishes the canal enters the system at this point, flowing from the Bassin de St-Férréol, the large reservoir in the Montagne Noire. There is a route to the Bassin from here, but an alternative excursion is offered at the end of Stage 2.

# STAGE 2
*Port Lauragais to Carcassonne*

| | |
|---|---|
| **Distance** | 54km excluding detours and excursion |
| **Path** | Gravel and hard clay: narrow and very difficult in some places; for final 1.5km approaching Carcassonne may need to use road; shares road on approach to Castalnaudary |
| **Shade** | Very good but some stretches exposed; take precautions |
| **Descent** | 77m |
| **Map** | 64 IGN *Carte de Promenade* |
| **Detours** | To Castelnaudary, Bram, Villesèquelande and Pezens |
| **Excursion** | From Guerre lock to St-Férréol reservoir (58km) |

This section of the canal starts at the Océan lock and passes close to the Montagne Noire, through the port town of Castelnaudary, the circular town of Bram, and the extraordinary fortified old town of Carcassonne.

**Cross to the south bank** at **Océan lock**. ▶

Cross to the south bank.

### Leaving Port Lauragais
The next stretch of the canal, along the shaded south bank past rolling countryside to Castelnaudary, is one of the most tranquil. The track is clay and typical of what is encountered on the descent to the Mediterranean. The path is in very poor condition immediately after Océan lock. Heavy rain has exposed roots and created large puddles, while animals and the wash from passing boats have undermined the bank. Take care on this section (note that it does improve quickly).

After 2.5km, reach the port of **Le Ségala** where a restaurant offers wine tasting. The path narrows after the port; there is an alternative broader clay path, although the surface becomes stonier approaching **Méditerrannée lock**. The towpath becomes broader too.

*Cycling the Canal du Midi*

## Stage 2: Port Lauragais to Carcassonne

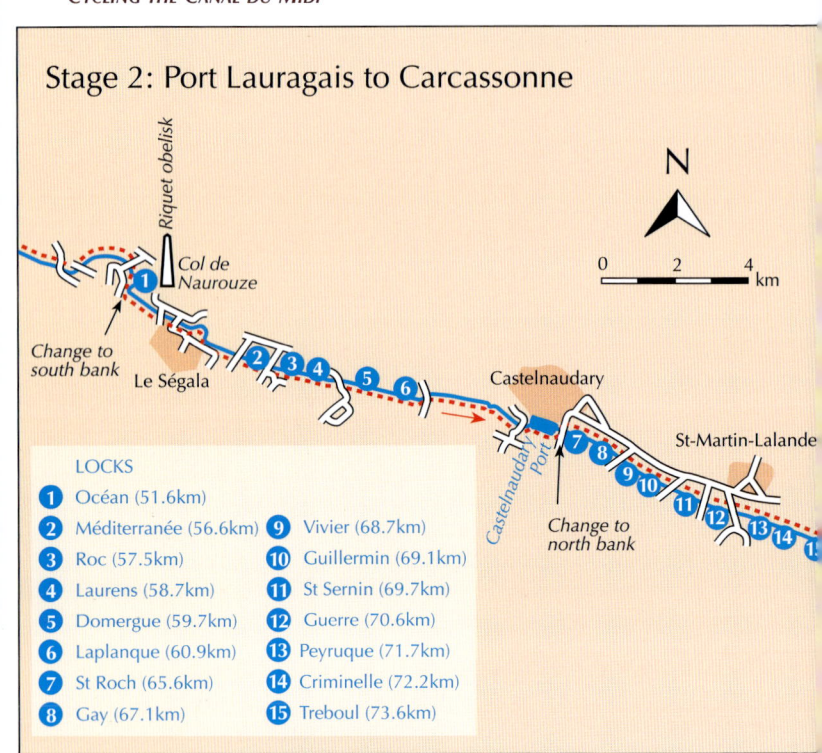

**LOCKS**
1. Océan (51.6km)
2. Méditerranée (56.6km)
3. Roc (57.5km)
4. Laurens (58.7km)
5. Domergue (59.7km)
6. Laplanque (60.9km)
7. St Roch (65.6km)
8. Gay (67.1km)
9. Vivier (68.7km)
10. Guillermin (69.1km)
11. St Sernin (69.7km)
12. Guerre (70.6km)
13. Peyruque (71.7km)
14. Criminelle (72.2km)
15. Treboul (73.6km)

map continues on page 70

**Roc lock** follows shortly after Méditerrannée. Roc is double-chambered, allowing boats ascend or descend a greater height; this section of the canal drops relatively quickly. The path is wide and easy to cycle. The next lock, **Laurens**, is triple-chambered and has a drop of close to 7m. **Domergue lock** is a little over 1km further on, as is the next lock, **Laplanque**.

The path joins a road for the short run into **Castelnaudary**; take care. The path and road diverge at the town; pass under the bridge to reach Castelnaudary's impressive port. To enter the town proper, climb to the road and follow it north.

## STAGE 2 – PORT LAURAGAIS TO CARCASSONNE

### DETOUR TO CASTELNAUDARY

*Castelnaudary port*

This is a major port, with over 7 hectares of open water, and represents one of Riquet's great achievements. It is a base for one of the major companies offering boats for hire on the canal, the Crown Blue Line.

The town reflects the wealth generated by the canal and the surrounding countryside. There are wonderful spacious squares, and many houses and public buildings dating from the centuries following the canal's opening.

There is evidence of continuous settlement here from Iron Age times. As was common in the area **Castelnaudry** was taken and retaken by armies that crossed and recrossed the Lauragais Plain, and became capital of the Lauragais region in 1477. Catherine de Médici established it as a Presidium (meeting place of a governing committee or council), and the foundation of a college in 1572 added to the town's prestige.

Castelnaudary is easy to explore on bike or on foot. The key tourist attractions are the Collégiale St-Michel dating from the 13th century, the 18th-century Chapelle Notre Dame de Pitié, and Cugarel's mill, which has now been restored. There are plenty of shops, restaurants, hotels and services such as pharmacies, doctors and a hospital. Castelnaudary's port is also well worth exploring, with shops, old warehouses and wine emporia on its northern quay

The regional dish *cassoulet* is one of the town's main claims to fame. The townspeople devised this stew while under siege from the English army during the Hundred Years' War (1337–1453). Along with haricot beans – ▶

## CYCLING THE CANAL DU MIDI

◀ the key ingredient – cassoulet typically includes *confits de canard*, pork, sausages and just about anything edible to hand. All restaurants offer their own *cassoulet* – each chef has his or her own version – and you can buy it canned or in jars.

Return to the canal path.

*Cross to the north bank.*

Follow the path and then road along the port's southern quays. Circumvent Crown Blue Line's dock before climbing to a bridge at **St Roch lock**. Cross the bridge and **change sides to the northern bank**. This road is dangerous; dismount before climbing to the bridge. ◀

> Four-chambered **St Roch lock** has one of the greatest drops in height (or rises) on the canal: 9.5m. The rapid flow of water was once used to power the wheels of watermills (no longer in use). Thomas Jefferson, who became third president of the United States, studied St Roch's lock system as part of his exploration of the canal as a model for one linking the Potomac river to Lake Erie.

There is a water tap on the wall of a building beside the lock.

A short stretch on tarmac follows, before the path reverts to a dirt track with some stones, which is easy to cycle. The N113, a main road from Castelnaudary to Carcassonne, runs alongside the canal, but is barely noticeable once the town's outskirts are left behind.

*For details of an excursion from Guerre lock to St-Férréol reservoir, see the end of Stage 2.*

Five locks are passed over the next 5km: **Gay**, **Vivier**, **Guillermin**, **St Sernin** and **Guerre**. There are good views of the Montagne Noire (Black Mountain) to the north along this path. Watch for a fairytale cottage set among the trees on the south bank shortly after you quit Castelnaudary. ◀

The lock-keepers' cottages are occupied and you pass very close to them; a notice at Guerre lock asks people not to stop outside the door.

## STAGE 2 – PORT LAURAGAIS TO CARCASSONNE

Follow the towpath on the northern side to reach **Peyruque lock** after 1km. The lock-keeper's house has a shop selling local produce, refreshments and ceramic goods. The GR7 leaves the canal path for St-Martin-Lalande just after the lock. Continue on to the next one, **Criminelle lock**.

The path joins a road and crosses an aqueduct before passing behind the lock-keeper's house at the **Treboul lock**. **Villepinte lock** is 4km further on. There is a small picnic area on the south bank at the bridge before this lock, and the village of the same name is 1km to the north of the canal.

**Sauzens lock** is another 1.7 km along the track. The path from Sauzens lock forks; take the one nearer the canal. Go around the lock-keeper's house at **Bram lock** (rather than through the garden). Just afterwards there is a *chambre d'hôte* with a gate opening onto the canal. Bram port is 600m after the lock.

Boats can be hired in Bram port. A restaurant/café, open during the tourist season, and a *chambre d'hôte* can be found over the bridge on the south side. A *relais*-style hotel, Chez Alain, is 500m to the north on the RN113. It has simple rooms and offers a set lunch and evening meal.

*View of the canal from St Roch lock in Castelnaudary*

*CYCLING THE CANAL DU MIDI*

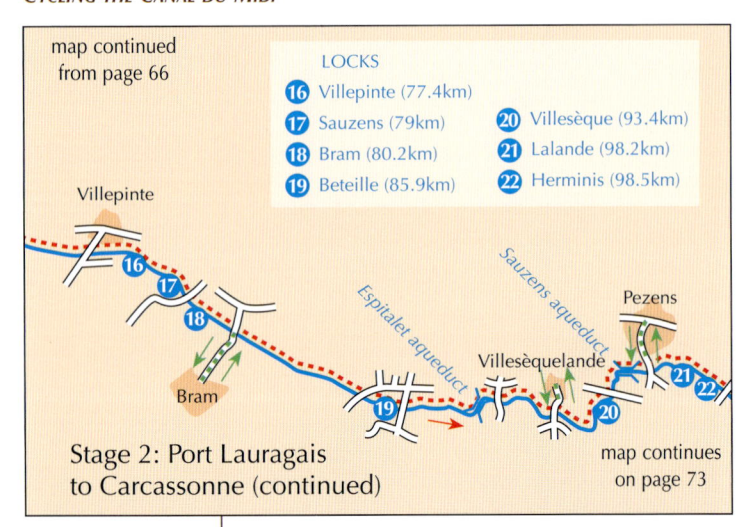

map continued from page 66

**LOCKS**
- 16 Villepinte (77.4km)
- 17 Sauzens (79km)
- 18 Bram (80.2km)
- 19 Beteille (85.9km)
- 20 Villesèque (93.4km)
- 21 Lalande (98.2km)
- 22 Herminis (98.5km)

Stage 2: Port Lauragais to Carcassonne (continued)

map continues on page 73

### DETOUR TO BRAM

Take the road south at Bram port to reach the town of **Bram**. The old town is circular, with the church at its centre. The streets are circular, with linking streets, a layout common in the old quarters of towns in the region and which formed part of the town's defences. Bram's church dates from the 14th century, and the château de Lordat from the 17th century. The town's archaeological museum is open all year. Bram was the site of one of the worst atrocities carried out during the persecution of the Cathars (see Introduction).

Return to the canal path.

Continue on the towpath on the northern bank of the canal for 5km towards Beteille lock, with good views of the countryside to the north. The railway track also runs close to the canal on the northern side. Cross the Rebenty river after 2.5km. The aqueduct is an arched stone construction, and there's a good view of it from the river's bank. Shortly after this pass under a railway bridge; 800m later come to a road bridge. Take the track

*Stage 2 – Port Lauragais to Carcassonne*

to the left and climb to the road. Turn right at the top and return to the canal track. The road north leads to Alzonne.

Continue to **Beteille lock**. Approximately 1km after crossing the **Espitalet aqueduct** the track comes to a bridge and briefly joins a road 3km further on. This road leads to the small village of **Villesèquelande** about 1km away.

### DETOUR TO VILLESÈQUELANDE

**Villesèquelande** is an attractive little village, with a small restaurant and grocery store. Note the old church and the presbytery dating from the 12th century (it is possible to visit the latter). The well in front of the presbytery is worth noting.

Return to the canal path.

Continue towards **Villesèque lock**. From here on the canal takes a meandering route towards Carcassonne. Under 1km later cross a main road; immediately after this the village of Sauzens appears on the opposite bank. The path divides shortly afterwards with the upper path giving good views of villages and the surrounding countryside. At 2.5km from Villesèque lock come to a small bridge and road. You will have already seen the town of **Pezens** to the north; leave the canal here if you want to visit it.

### DETOUR TO PEZENS

Follow the road northwards from the bridge. Pass the railway bridge and continue straight to the N113 junction. Any of the roads opposite enter **Pezens** old town.

This lovely old town is dissected by the busy N113, with most of the older part on its northern side. The town dates from at least the 13th century and retains some old fortifications and a town gate in good repair. The church of St-Jean dates from the 14th century and dominates the old quarter, but the small streets and alleyways are also well worth exploring. ▶

*Old gate into Pezens*

◀ You find the old town gate by following the narrow street that leaves the eastern corner of the church square. Note a marble plaque on the left wall of a building approximately halfway along the street, describing how the Château Pezens was given to the diocesan congregation of the sacred family to educate the local girls. The community closed its doors in 2004.

The gate is best viewed from outside the town. However, don't miss a small statue of the Blessed Virgin above it on the town side; such statues are common above town entrances. As you pass through the gate you'll note seats on either side. Once outside the walls you can view the fortifications, including an intact tower built into the town walls close to the gate.

There are a few shops, cafés and restaurants on the main street. Return to the canal bridge.

Continue along the northern path towards **Lalande lock**. There is a sign pointing to the Domaine Lalande 500m to the north.

### THE DOMAINE LALANDE

The Domaine Lalande offers wine for sale or tasting. The local climate enables producers to grow a wide variety of grapes. The Cabardès appellation, the region's AOC, is the only one in France where producers blend a minimum of 40 percent of Atlantic grapes (such as Merlot or Cabernet Sauvignon) with a minimum of 40 percent Mediterranean grapes (Syrah and Grenache). It is the point at which the warm humid conditions of the Bordeaux area meet the drier and hotter Mediterranean climate. This may explain the frequent thunderstorms that affect this part of the canal all year round.

## STAGE 2 – PORT LAURAGAIS TO CARCASSONNE

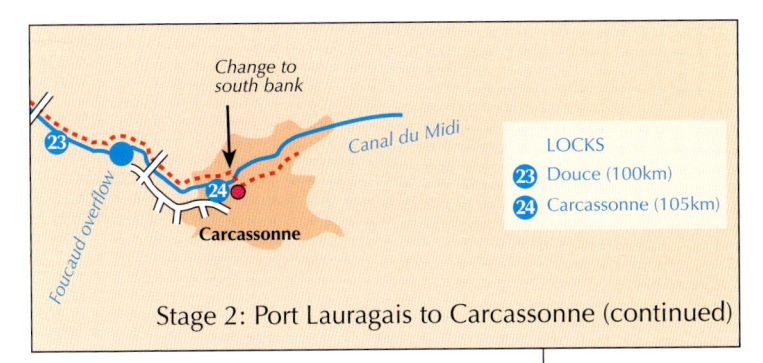

**Stage 2: Port Lauragais to Carcassonne (continued)**

LOCKS
23 Douce (100km)
24 Carcassonne (105km)

Lalande is a double lock and is quickly followed by **Herminis lock** 270m later. There is a *crêperie* at the lock-keeper's house (in season); the Mirage Barge offering bed and breakfast also moors here in season. Cycle a further 1.37km to **Douce lock**, and **Épanchoir de Focaud** (Focaud overflow) a further 1.7km onwards. This represents the beginning of the canal to Carcassonne. Originally, Carcassonne's town council refused to pay for the canal to pass through their town, but changed their tune when they saw the success the canal brought to other towns. The Épanchoir represents the point where the canal diverted to Carcassonne.

On the approach to Carcassonne the canal passes through a deep cutting with steep banks on either side; the path deteriorates and narrows, becomes mucky and is prone to erosion. Turn back and follow the road into the town if the path is blocked or proves too difficult. It can be rejoined at Carcassonne port opposite the railway station. The canal path passes under a tall viaduct before the town. Local drunks sometimes congregate under the final bridge before the port, so avoid cycling this section in late evening or early morning.

### Carcassonne

It takes a day to explore Carcassonne properly. Those who haven't visited it before should think about spending a night here – if only to see the Cité lit against the night sky.

map continued from page 70

Its Bastille night (14 July) fireworks are famous and probably the best in all France. Those planning to stop here in high summer should book accommodation in advance.

There are two distinct parts to Carcassonne: the lower town and the Cité, the ancient walled town. The lower town offers the best value for restaurants, hotels, bed and breakfasts, and general provisions. The Cité is the main tourist attraction in the area (if not the region).

The lower town owes its origins to the Count of Toulouse, Trencavel. He attempted to regain his titles and domains in 1239. He laid siege to Carcassonne with help from some locals but was forced to withdraw on the arrival of an army sent by the king of France, Louis IX (also known as St Louis). Louis punished the population living around the Cité's wall for their alleged support of Trencavel. He ordered them to live on the other bank of the river – the site of the present lower town, the **Bastide St Louis**.

The lower town is designed on a grid structure and easy to explore. It retains its original bastide (fortified town) layout with **Place Carnot** in the middle as the town's main square. To reach it from the canal, cross the bridge and follow Rue G. Clemenceau to reach the square, with a Neptune fountain its main feature. The square is lined with cafés and restaurants and is the location for regular markets.

Boulevards have replaced the town's original fortifications. Sights include the cathedral (**St Michel**) and **St Vincent's** church, relics of the two original town parishes. The Musée des Beaux Arts has a collection of paintings from the 17th to 19th centuries.

**Place Gambetta** is a large square close to the Aude river and the **Pont Neuf** (new bridge). The square is busy, but worth visiting for its architecture.

### The Cité

You can cycle to the fortified Cité from the lower town (about 2km); the best view is from the **Pont Vieux** (old bridge). Take the **Rue du Pont Vieux** from the southwestern corner of Place Gambetta and follow it towards the

*Stage 2 – Port Lauragais to Carcassonne*

bridge. Continue straight ahead after crossing the bridge and follow **Rue Trivalle**, taking the third turn on the right onto **Rue G. Nadaud** until you reach **Port Narbonnaise** (Narbonne Gate), the main entrance and widest gate into the fortified town.

The streets of the Cité are cobbled, pedestrianised and, in summer, very crowded. It's probably best to lock

*The Cité at Carcassonne*

*The Narbonne Gate*

## CYCLING THE CANAL DU MIDI

*The old bridge in Carcassonne*

your bike securely and go around on foot. As you enter note the large bailey, Les Lices, between the defensive walls. Knights used this area for jousting competitions and military drilling. The tourist office is on the right as you enter Port Narbonnaise, and will provide a free street map.

The Cité site has been occupied since before Roman times. It came under the control of each wave of invaders and was strengthened and extended. It reached its zenith in the 12th and early 13th centuries when it was the capital of the region and under the control of the viscount of Carcassonne. The crusaders captured it in the 1209 and the knight Simon de Montfort became viscount.

The town declined after the treaty of the Pyrenees (1659) when Roussillon became part of the French kingdom, and thus lost its strategic importance. It fell into disrepair and was inhabited by the poor; its buildings supplied a source of stone for construction works in the locality. A local architect, Jean Pierre Cros Mayrevieille, campaigned for the restoration of the Cité as a national monument. The French government agreed and the reconstruction began in the 1840s.

The town is reputed to have taken its name from Carcas, widow of the Muslim prince Balaak, who held the fort in the 8th century and died in a skirmish with the Emperor Charlemagne. However, his wife donned his livery and continued to lead his army. Carcas organised the defence of the town during a prolonged siege. With her army greatly depleted, Carcas ordered her forces to make straw men to create the impression that the battlements were still guarded. When the town's food rations were reduced to a pig and a bag of wheat, she ordered that the pig be fed the wheat grains. She then hurled the gorged pig at the feet of Charlemagne's soldiers. On seeing this Charlemagne was convinced that the town was so well provisioned that they could afford to feed their pigs grain, and he lifted the siege. It is said that the church bells rang for the victory, giving rise to the shout 'Carcas sonne' – 'Carcas rings' – and thus the name Carcassonne. A reproduction of a stone carving of Carcas can be found on the right-hand pillar beside the bridge leading into Port Narbonnaise. The original is in the château inside.

The key sights inside the Cité include the **Château Comptal**, **Basilique St Nazaire**, the walls, battlements (and the views from these) and the small medieval streets and squares.

The château is a fort within the town's fortifications. Follow the main street from Port Narbonnaise, **Rue Cros Maryrevieille**, to the **Place du Château**. There is a charge to visit the château but it is well worth the cost. Enter through the castle's main gate and cross a bridge to the main courtyard. The tour of the castle follows a first-floor landing and leads around the outer battlements. There are especially good views to the north of the city towards the Montagne Noire. Some of the towers replace earlier Roman ones; the medieval rooms now house a collection of sculptures from the town and the Carcassonne region. Chief among these is a 14th-century statue of the smiling Madonna, probably the work of a Sienese artist.

The château is a venue for major concerts and operas during the summer festival; book early to be sure of getting a ticket for the popular events. The château also provides a space for modern art exhibitions and installations.

The **cathedral of Sts Nazarius and Celsus** is in the southwestern corner of the Cité, a wonderful (if now highly modified) structure. Only the nave survives from the original 11th-century church; most of the remainder

*Interior of the cathedral of St Nazarius and St Celsus*

dates from the 13th and 14th centuries. The stained glass windows are among the best examples of their type and depict, amongst other things, St Celsus presenting her son, St Nazarius. The light from the rose windows imbues the interior with delicate colours.

There are tombs of bishops and other notaries throughout the church, and a tombstone with the inscription Simon de Montfort. However, the body is no longer buried beneath as his son exhumed it and moved it to Montfort l'Amaury.

Before leaving, be sure to turn and take a look at the organ at the end of the church. It's easy to miss this as your eye is drawn towards the main body of the church on entry.

## EXCURSION
*from Guerre lock to St-Férréol reservoir*

| | |
|---|---|
| **Distance** | 57km |
| **Path** | Road and track |
| **Shade** | Little shade during climb |
| **Climb** | 350m |
| **Map** | 64 IGN *Carte de Promenade* |

This excursion to the source of the Canal du Midi leads to the edge of the Montagne Noire, the last outcrop of the Massif Centrale. The route gives spectacular views over the plain and as far as the often snow-capped Pyrenees. You cycle through woodland, historic villages, hidden valleys, farmland and mountain countryside to reach the reservoir, a centre for swimming and water sports.

The route has some steep climbs. Most of the cycle is on small roads, but part of it follows a marked long-distance walking route (GR7). There is relatively little shade and much of the route is on the southern face of hills and mountains. You may also experience high winds. In winter, the temperature drops noticeably during the climb from the canal (140m) to 490m at the reservoir. The road can become iced and snow-covered during severe cold snaps.

Leave the canal at Guerre lock. Head northwards on a small road (D116). Reach a crossroads with the large (and very busy) main road. Carry straight on towards the village of **St-Martin-Lalande**. Climb a slight incline to a cross and bear right following the main road into the village square, Place Leon Blum.

Note a house dating from the 18th century on the left-hand side of the square as you face the town hall. Take the road on the right out of the square. Pass an old gate on your left (Place du Pont-Levis) beside a 15th-century church. Follow the road as it bears left, passing a sewage works, and descends to a crossroads with a stop sign.

Go straight through the crossroads, passing a cross on the left and a sign for the GR on the right. Go over a bridge and at the next crossroads go straight through.

*Cycling the Canal du Midi*

Note a large turreted building on your left. Take a left turn following the GR sign (2.5km).

About 400m further on a track drops slightly to the right (see picture opposite). Take this track and almost immediately cross a small bridge. The path then swings left and climbs. Stop at the hillcrest and look back at what can be a spectacular view of the Pyrenees. Continue through oak woods for another 1km.

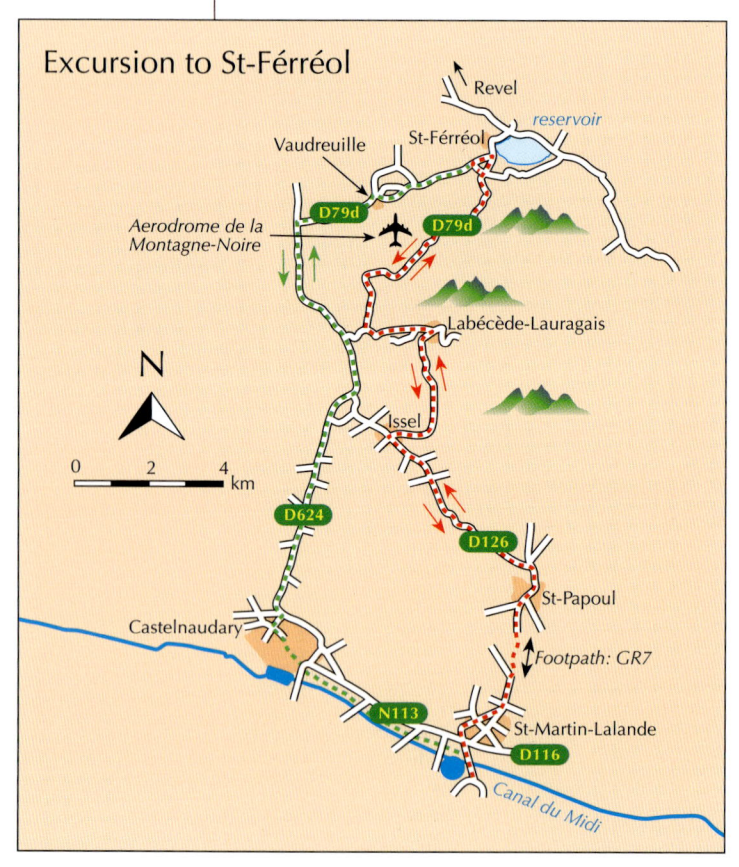

## Excursion to St-Férréol

## Excursion – from Guerre lock to St-Férréol reservoir

*Track dropping to the right on the GR7*

The track reaches a road (4.6km). Again, look back at the view before following the road to a T-junction. Turn right and continue towards the town of St-Papoul.

The 8th-century Benedictine abbey is the main attraction in **St-Papoul**. It's on the left and partially hidden behind other buildings. The cloisters, four galleries around a central square, are one of its most striking features. These can be seen through a gate on the left, or during a visit to the abbey. ▶

*An 18th-century house in St-Papoul*

> ◀ The abbey has featured significantly in the history of the area. Pope John XXII made it a bishopric in AD1317; the abbey was also used to imprison Cathars early in the 14th century, including Guillaume Vital. The abbot agreed to release him and 40 others if he paid a large ransom. Guillaume gathered the money but was double-crossed and robbed by the abbey's guards. He was probably burnt at the stake there later.
>
> The rest of the village is worth exploring. Much of it appears to have been left untouched since medieval times. Visit the old part (Cité) by crossing the road from the abbey and following the sign for the Mairie. Continue along this street and note the town gate at the end, another on the left, and the medieval houses.
>
> There is one café in the village, on the left on the Issel road past the abbey. It offers a set lunch and evening meals – all served in large portions.

Take the Issel road (D126) to continue the cycle to the reservoir, with great views south as you climb. Before reaching **Issel** (13km) the road branches: one branch leads to the village while the other heads for Labécéde-Lauragais. You may wish to visit Issel, a pleasant village with a lovely church beside a semi-circle of houses.

Follow the road for **Labécède-Lauragais**. Pass through this hamlet to reach a T-junction (17km). Turn left and just beyond the village take the right branch where the road forks, marked the Chemin Vieux. Continue on this road, straight at first but then with sharp turns, crossing an old bridge at the point of a hairpin bend. From this, a short climb leads to a junction (20km). Take the right turn (D334), following the signpost for the Aerodrome de la Montagne-Noire and Bassin de St-Férréol. You are now at approximately 400m elevation.

The road climbs through a very exposed landscape, passing the aerodrome on the left, before reaching the highest point of the day at just under 500m above sea level, with an excellent view of the reservoir. The road

## EXCURSION – FROM GUERRE LOCK TO ST-FÉRRÉOL RESERVOIR

drops quickly through a series of sharp bends to reach the reservoir (28km).

The **Bassin de St-Férréol** has an area of 70ha, and a dam 800m long. Note a bronze monument to Pierre Paul Riquet at the point where the road reaches the edge of the reservoir. Cycle around it and explore the surrounding countryside; there are large forests approximately 12km to the east, grouped under the title of the Forêt de la Montagne Noire. The next nearest town is Revel, 3.3km away, with services and facilities and a renowned centre for carpentry. You may wish to use St-Férréol or Revel as bases for exploring the surrounding countryside. There are campsites, hotels, cafés and restaurants near the lake, most of which are only open in the high season or at holiday times.

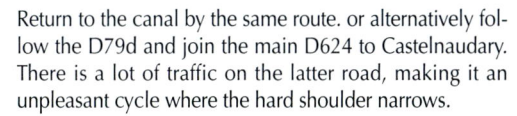

*Canal sign in St-Férréol*

Return to the canal by the same route. or alternatively follow the D79d and join the main D624 to Castelnaudary. There is a lot of traffic on the latter road, making it an unpleasant cycle where the hard shoulder narrows.

*St-Férréol reservoir*

*CYCLING THE CANAL DU MIDI*

# STAGE 3
## Carcassonne to Homps

| | |
|---|---|
| **Distance** | 40km excluding detours and excursions |
| **Path** | Gravel and clay: generally good |
| **Shade** | Overall good but exposed in parts; particular care needed where path runs on sunny side of trees |
| **Descent** | 63m |
| **Maps** | 64 and 72 IGN *Carte de Promenade* |
| **Detours** | To Marseillette rice farm and Étang de Marseillette |
| **Excursions** | From Trèbes to Lastours (42km) |
| | From Homps to Minerve (36km) |

From Carcassonne the canal path passes through the towns of Trèbes and Marseillette. The route runs alongside a large drained lake, now used for producing fruit, vegetables and rice. Mount Alaric can be seen at the edge of the plain as you cycle beside vineyards and farms. This stage includes the Argentdouble canal works – one of the wonders of the Canal du Midi – and ends in the attractive port of Homps.

### Leaving Carcassonne

Return to the canal at the bridge in front of Carcassonne railway station at **Port Marengo**. Follow the path on the canal's **south side – a change of banks**. ◄ The path is light gravel and easy to cycle. Watch for the last glimpse of the Cité on the south as you leave the town's suburbs and have the privilege of seeing two UNESCO heritage sites at the same time (the Canal du Midi and the Cité). The first lock encountered is that of **St Jean**, about 3km from Carcassonne port.

In less than 1km reach the **Pont Canal du Fresquel** (aqueduct) over the Fresquel river. This is an amazing piece of engineering with a lock at the end. The bridge has three arches; scramble down the embankment to get a better view of these. The aqueduct is 42.85m long and 26.3m high; dismount when crossing. The lock is

*Change to the south bank.*

84

*Stage 3 – Carcassonne to Homps*

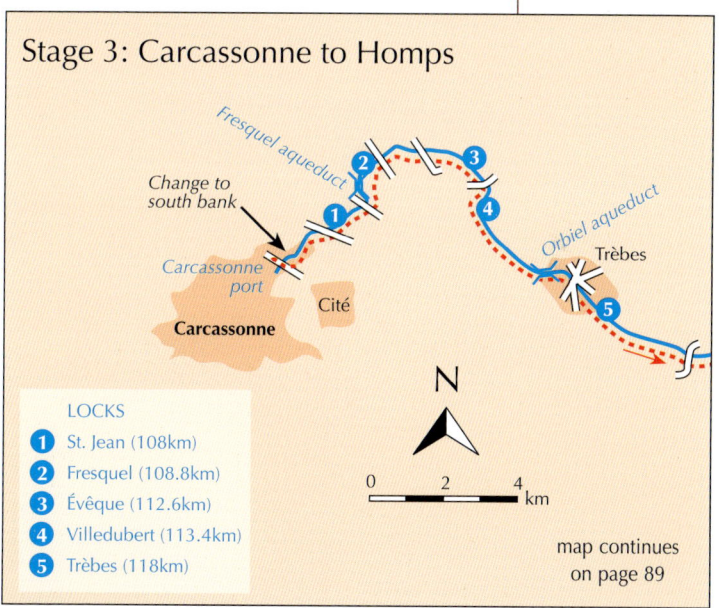

*Typical stone bridge located near the Orbiel crossing*

## Stage 3: Carcassonne to Homps

**LOCKS**
1. St. Jean (108km)
2. Fresquel (108.8km)
3. Évêque (112.6km)
4. Villedubert (113.4km)
5. Trèbes (118km)

map continues on page 89

double-chambered with a basin between it and the next, **Fresquel lock**. This construction marks the point where the Carcassonne Canal rejoins the Canal du Midi.

The path beside the locks descends steeply and is dressed with gravel; it can be slippery and cyclists can fall. Those with heavy bags should dismount.

Cross another stream a few hundred metres later, noting overflow systems and small irrigation canals along the way. The path degrades somewhat at this stage; watch out for roots as you pass through woodland. Pass **Évêque lock** next and, after crossing a road, continue on the south side. The path is now a track, still good quality but with less tree cover.

There is a small reservoir behind the lock-keeper's house at **Villedubert lock**. There are two paths at this point, an upper and lower; the upper is better quality, and the paths merge after 1km. The canal then passes through a cutting, with limited shade. Note a row of pine trees on the opposite bank.

*Trèbes lock*

## STAGE 3 – CARCASSONNE TO HOMPS

Reach a stone bridge, cross a road and continue on a tarmac track. Another canal branches to the north. The **Orbiel aqueduct** is reached, a large arched crossing. You can take a path down to the riverbank to view the aqueduct, one of the major river crossings along the length of the canal and built to deal with occasional flood torrents.

The port of **Trèbes** is almost immediately after the crossing. Join the road (Rue Riquet) here. Trèbes is a particularly busy town; take care at the junction leading to the port.

Trèbes port is very lively in summer, and attracts lots of people with campervans who park along the roadway beside the towpath. In season, there are restaurants open along the port with tables right beside the canal; watch out for waiters as you cycle through. This is a good place for a picnic. ▶

For details of an excursion from Trèbes to Lastours, see the end of Stage 3.

> **Trèbes** has one main attraction: the church of St Etienne, featuring painted wood from the 14th century. To reach it, turn right after the bridge and follow Rue 11 November to it. Pass an English bookshop and internet café on the street. The church faces towards Mount Alaric and its surrounding peaks.
>
> There is a tourist office beside the canal, an ATM and a post office, and plenty of shops in the town. The Aude river flows through the town; follow the road south and you'll come to the main bridge over the river.

Continue on the south bank; the path is gravel and easy to cycle. **Trèbes lock**, a three-chambered lock with two watermills, is 400m east of the town. There is a restaurant, the Moulin de Trèbes, on the bank opposite. Mount Alaric comes into view to the south at the next bridge.

The canal meanders through lovely countryside passing a château on the opposite bank (a wooden bridge leads to it). Another bridge over the canal leads to a religious institute at Millegrand; Millegrand caveau (wine producer) is behind the institute. Later, take a double bridge over a small stream. The path becomes more gravelly at this point.

Marseillette bridge is reached 9km after Trèbes lock. The town of **Marseillette** is south of the canal, and dates back to the time of the Gauls. Little remains from that period although there are some remains of the fortifications. Note an old gate into the town on the main road.

*Optical telegraph tower in Marseillette*

The clock tower, originally a relay station for an optical telegraph network, is **Marseillette**'s most prominent feature. An ex-priest, Claude Chappée, invented the system in the 18th century, and Napoleon was interested in this revolutionary new communications system. Built in 1834, the tower was part of the network linking Montpellier to Toulouse. The technology suffered from certain shortcomings, especially in daylight and bad weather. The tower was barely finished when Morse code and electric telegraphy were invented, rendering the optical system obsolete.

The small church of St André dating from the 12th century can be found down a little road on the opposite side of the main road to the clock tower. The church faces towards the Alaric Mountains and has excellent views.

***Stage 3 – Carcassonne to Homps***

## Stage 3: Carcassonne to Homps (continued)

map continued from page 85

*drained lake*

*Jouarres lake*

*Argentdouble overflow*

*Aiguille aqueduct*

*Millegrand aqueduct*

Olonzac

Homps

Laredorte

Change to south bank

St. Gabriel

Puichéric

Marseillette

Change to north bank

**LOCKS**
- 6 Marseillette (127.2km)
- 7 Fonfile (130.4km)
- 8 St Martin (131.6km)
- 9 Aiguille (133.3km)
- 10 Puichéric (136.3km)
- 11 Jouarres (142.7km)

0   2   4 km

---

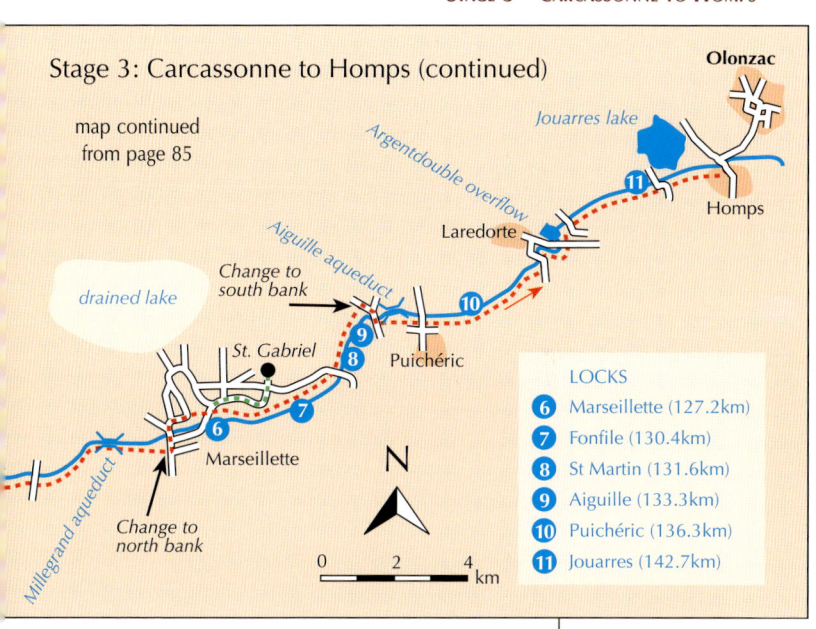

The path **changes to the northern side at Marseillette bridge.** ▶ **Marseillette lock** is approximately 1km further east. You can make a detour onto the Étang de Marseillette (Marseillette Lagoon), also known as the Étang Asséchée (Dried or Drained Lagoon).

Change to the north bank.

### DETOUR TO ÉTANG DE MARSEILLETTE

This drained lake in a natural hollow beside the canal was originally 9km long and 6.5km wide and covered 2000ha. Henry IV ordered it to be drained at the end of the 16th century, a difficult project that took over 250 years to achieve. Anne Marie Coppinger, an Irish woman who had settled in France, convinced Emperor Napoleon to complete the work.

The land is fertile and produces a wide variety of fruit, vegetables and rice. To visit the drained lake and the rice producer (6km round trip), take the tarmac road north (to the left as you travel from Carcassonne to Homps). ▶

*CYCLING THE CANAL DU MIDI*

*St Gabriel château, where rice is produced*

◀ Note a sign for the Étang Asséchée. Reach a T-junction in a few hundred metres; turn right and follow the signs for **St Gabriel**. You are now cycling along the edge of the old lake; note drainage canals beside the road. Continue on the road as it bears left, with the château straight ahead, a tall, turreted, white building with a grey tiled roof. Enter the château yard to find a small office in the row of buildings on the left, where you can buy rice grown on the lakebed.

It's easy to explore the surrounding countryside. Apart from Marseillette, villages around the lake include Aigues-Vives, St-Frichoux, St-Roch and Puichéric. There is little shade on the lakeside.

Return to the canal by the same route.

## STAGE 3 – CARCASSONNE TO HOMPS

From Marseillette lock continue on the towpath on the northern side. Look out for the château St Gabriel to the north in the distance. The three-chambered **Fonfile lock** is 3.3km further on. **St Martin lock** is reached 1.2km later, a double lock with a flight of steps on each side of the main lock gate. Note the **St Martin aqueduct** shortly after the lock. The path is rough and narrow as the next lock, **Aiguille**, is approached.

Aiguille is a double lock, home to a range of wood carvings and sculptures and a picnic spot. A notice, in French, gives details of the Marseillette Lagoon and gives an idea of its scale – you have been passing through reclaimed land since leaving Marseillette Lock.

**Change to the south side** at Aiguille lock. ▶ Cross another aqueduct within 0.5km. Shortly, note the village of **Puichéric** on the right, which can be visited by taking the road at the next bridge. The lock of the same name is a double one and comes approximately 1km after the bridge.

Next, reach the bridge that leads to the village of **Laredorte**, 3.5km after Puicheric lock. This has a small port with a restaurant, le Rivassel, on the north bank.

Continue on the south bank for a further 1km. **Ouvrages de l'Argentdouble**, an 11-arched cobblestone bridge, is one of the wonders of the Canal du Midi. Built in 1693, it allows excess water to fall from the canal into the Argentdouble river. The best view of this is obtained

Change to the south bank.

*The Argentdouble spillover*

when approaching from the north; 300m later you cross the river itself on another bridge, built in 1688, and which copes with rapid currents when the river is in full flood. About 0.25km later pass the Logement du Garde du Canal where the post barges stopped for food.

**Jouarres lock**, 3km from the Ouvrages de l'Argentdouble, is single-chambered with a large drop. The track is of variable quality at this stage, and is gravelly just after the lock. Cross another body of water shortly after it and cycle around a small harbour or inlet, then cross a deep, stagnant drain. Jouarres wine producers have an outlet 100m south of the canal, offering tastings and sales. Continue to **Homps** port.

### Homps and Olonzac

The two towns are almost joined; there is a mere 300m between them. **Homps** is a good place to spend a night, and a suitable base for exploring the surrounding countryside. The town has shops, restaurants, post office, cybercafé and the usual services. Both port and village are attractive and bustling during the summer. The Auberge de l'Arbousier is a pleasant hotel and restaurant on the canal's south bank beside the port. Vineyards surround the village, which lies in the Minerve wine-growing area.

**St Etienne's chapel**, dating from the 14th century, is also on the south bank. It is easy to find as there is public parking in its grounds and it is signed. One château nearby, which belonged to the Knights of Malta, is worth a look. You can see into the courtyard through a railed gate.

**Joarres lake** is close to the town on the north side, and is reached by following the road to Olonzac and taking a left turn (signposted) outside the village. A watersports centre operates there in summer, with swimming and sailboarding.

**Olonzac** is another busy little town with all necessary services. It traces its history back to the Iron Age, but there is little obvious evidence of its rich history apart from some Roman remains, and it has an archaeological museum. It has a very good all-year-round market on Tuesdays. ◄

For details of an excursion from Homps to Minerve, see the end of Stage 3 below.

## EXCURSION
*from Trèbes to Lastours*

| | |
|---|---|
| **Distance** | 42km |
| **Path** | Road and track: very stony in parts on GR36 |
| **Shade** | Very exposed |
| **Climb** | 154m |
| **Maps** | 64 and 72 IGN *Carte de Promenade* |
| **Walk** | Castles at Lastours can only be accessed on foot (exposed 100m climb) |

This excursion follows the Orbeil river valley to the towers of Lastours (or Cabardès). It is possible to climb to 300m above sea level and use part of the long-distance footpath GR36 for some of the return route.

In Trèbes, cross the bridge going north. Take a left turn following Avenue Pierre Loti to a roundabout. Turn left onto the Route du Cabardès (D101). Stick to this road – note it can be quite busy. After 6km take a right turn onto another busy road, Avenue Jean Jaurès, at a crossroads in **Villalier**.

**Villalier** was once the location of a large château which was sadly demolished in the 18th century, and the stones used to build a hotel in Carcassonne. The five-storey church tower dates from the 19th century and dominates the village. Villalier is the resting place of the 19th-century republican revolutionary, d'Armand Barbès (1809–70). He was prominent in the workers' movement in France, leading unsuccessful revolts before dying in voluntary exile in the Netherlands.

The village has a grocery store and other services. It has several outlets selling wine directly.

## Excursion to Lastours

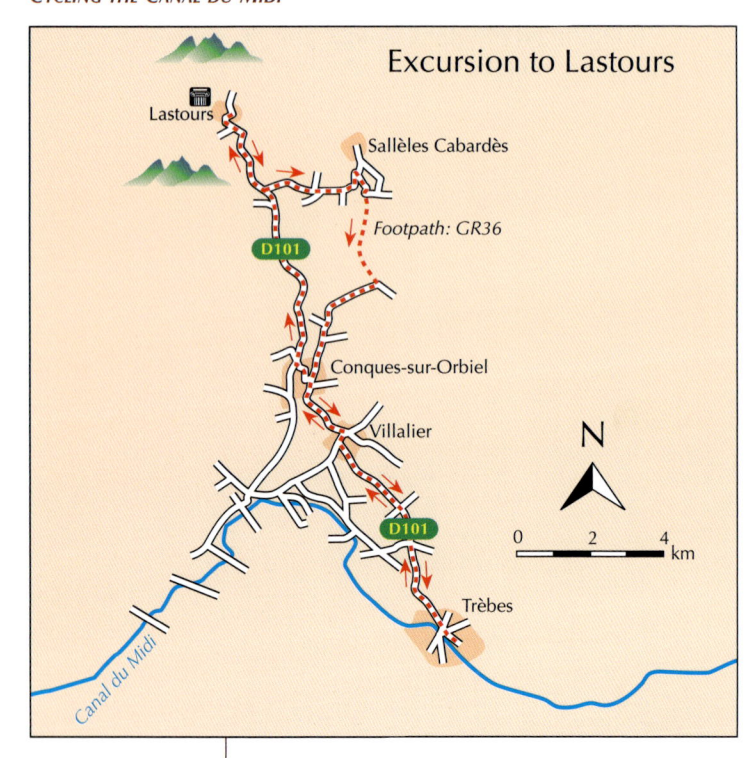

Leave the village still following the D101, Avenue de la Montagne Noire, towards **Conques-sur-Orbiel** (a further 2km). Approach the village on the Avenue Barbès and follow the one-way system into the village centre.

> **Conques-sur-Orbiel** is an old medieval village, but there has probably been a settlement here since 5000BC. There are the remains of an old castle and its defences, and St-Michel church probably dates back to Roman times. The village has shops and a café near the bridge over the Orbiel river.

## EXCURSION – FROM TRÈBES TO LASTOURS

*Church in Conques-sur-Orbiel*

Continue on the D101, on Avenue de la Fleur de Lys, and cross the bridge over the Orbiel river. Turn right and follow the road signposted for Lastours for approximately 8km. Pass a quarry on your left; note a bridge built of bicycles on your right shortly before Lastours.

On reaching **Lastours** cycle to the end of the village; cars have to be left at the entrance. Look out for a tall chimneystack to the right of the main road – a remnant of a disused mine – and for the Lastours castles on the hill above. The entrance to the castles is close to a restaurant, Le Puits du Trésor, which also has a bar selling sandwiches. The village has several cafés and restaurants.

*CYCLING THE CANAL DU MIDI*

> Lock your bike to the railings in front of the visitor centre where tickets to visit the **Lastours castles** (€5 at the time of writing) are purchased, then climb on foot up a steep stony path to the ruins.
>
> There is evidence to suggest that the site has been occupied since AD500. The grave of a young girl dating from that time was found in 1961 and she became known as the Princess of Lastours. Objects influenced by Egyptian and Mycean cultures were also found, indicating that the residents at that time traded widely.
>
> There are four castles: Cabaret, Tour Régine, Surdespine and Quertinheux. The Cabardès family controlled the region in the 10th century and probably built Cabaret, Surdespine and Quertinheux in the following century. The castles and village were Cathar strongholds and resisted crusader attacks until 1229. The village and towers were destroyed as a retaliatory act but rebuilt subsequently; the Tour Régine was added later.
>
> The castles became an administrative centre for the region until the French Revolution, were declared historical monuments in 1905 and restored. Archaeological digs have revealed evidence of the earlier castles and settlements, and these are passed as you climb the hill. The ruins are fragile, and it is forbidden to walk on walls or remove any objects.

To return to Trèbes, leave the village by the same road you used to enter it. After 2km come to a junction and turn left, following signs for Sallèles Carbadès on the D111. Cross a bridge and climb out of the Orbeil valley. At a crossroads continue towards Sallèles Carbadès (elevation 250m). Arrive at a junction with **Sallèles Carbadès** village visible 300m to the north.

Cycle in the direction of Villeneuve Minervois for 400m. Pass a graveyard on your right. Turn right at an iron cross beside the local recycling centre and descend a tarmac road that degrades to a clay track (now following part of GR36). Cross a stone bridge and then pass a

## EXCURSION – FROM TRÈBES TO LASTOURS

*View of the Lastours castles*

sign for Forêt Communale de Villegly. The path is stony for a few hundred metres and difficult to cycle without wide tyres; walk if necessary. On reaching a tarmac road turn right and cycle through vineyards back to Conques-sur-Orbeil. Climb into the village on Avenue Montagne Noire with public football pitches on your right. Take a right branch at a fork in the road; at the next junction turn left, followed by a right at another fork. Drop quickly to a main road and follow this to the church.

Return to the canal at Trèbes using the D101.

*Cycling the Canal du Midi*

**EXCURSION**

*from Homps to Minerve*

| | |
|---|---|
| **Distance** | 36km |
| **Path** | Tarmac road |
| **Shade** | Very exposed, little useful shade while cycling |
| **Climb** | 190m |
| **Map** | 72 IGN *Carte de Promenade* |

This excursion climbs through the fertile plain flanking the canal to the dramatic gorges of the Cesse river. Visit Cesseras and Azillanet before reaching the Cathar stronghold of Minerve, perched precariously above the Cesse gorge. Your efforts are rewarded with excellent views of the hills and plain. The route descends to the circular village of Aigne, and the fort towns of Beaufort and Oupia, before returning to Olonzac.

Cross the bridge to the north bank of the canal at **Homps** and follow the road (D2610) to Olonzac. Enter the town and then take the D10 towards Minerve. A few hundred metres outside the town you come to a left turn signposted for Cesseras. Follow this road and then turn right (onto the D182) at a crossroads towards Cesseras, visible in the distance (7.9km from Homps). Follow this road across a plain lined with vineyards. The best view of Château **Cesseras** is from the road as you approach the village.

Stay on the road until, after a small hill, a bigger road is reached (the D168, which changes to the D4 close by). Cross the road to enter the village's old centre.

> **Cesseras** has a long history. Nearby caves have yielded evidence of Cro-Magnon man, and dolmens in the region indicate prehistoric settlements. Pierre Raymond, Lord of Cesseras, was executed for heresy during the war against the Cathars. The streets are ▶

### EXCURSION – FROM HOMPS TO MINERVE

◀ narrow with good examples of the typical architecture encountered in the Minerve area, with archways leading into courtyards or small alleys. Climb up to find Place St Genies with its 15th-century church, and take a walk around the château's walls and ramparts, which are impressive if somewhat run down. The village has a shop and a café.

Leave the village on the main road D168 (D4) heading east for **Azillanet**, a little under 2km away. Take the left fork in the road on the D168 (E7), following a sign for

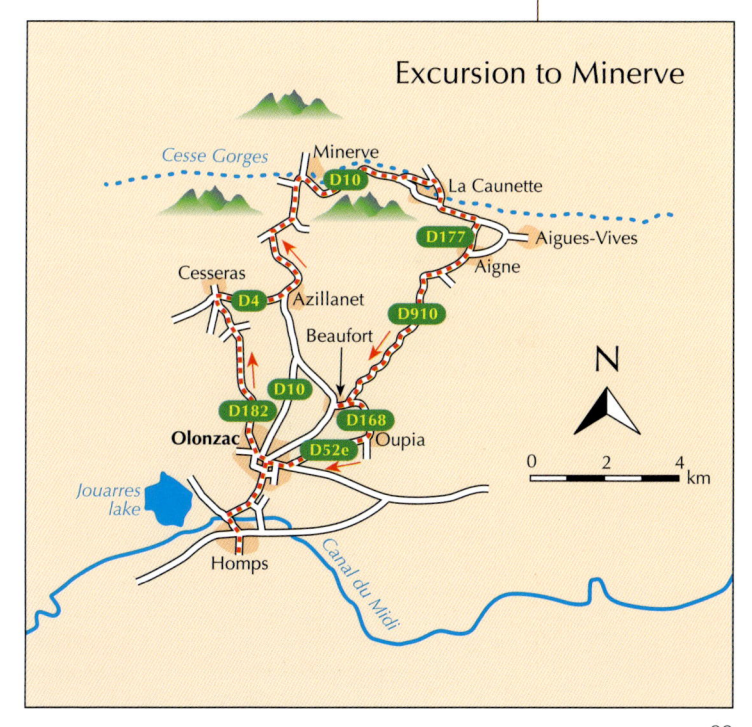

*On the road to Azillanet*

Minerve La Caunette. The road climbs through Azillanet to reach the church of St Laurent at 108m altitude. From the church square note the village's narrow streets and arches; there are also the remains of an old château and parts of what was once a convent. Some of the houses are in poor repair, giving the town an authentic (if ramshackle) feel.

From the small roundabout outside the church take the road left that climbs towards Minerve 4.5km away. This climb is steep and brings you on to a south-facing road with full exposure to the sun. Reach a picnic/parking spot on the left-hand side of the road 1.5km from the village. There are great views across the plain and, on a good day, the Pyrenees in the south.

Continue to climb between the mountains reaching an elevation of 240m – the highest point on this excursion. Round the mountain and come to the **River Cesse gorges**. These spectacular gorges are steep-sided and studded with caves and crevices. Descend quickly towards **Minerve**.

Minerve (elevation 190m) is perched on top of a cliff above the Cesse gorge on the south and the Briant river gorge on the north. Pass the road to the left with signposts for parking. Continue until you see an arched stone bridge and cross it to reach the village. The bridge gives an excellent view of the village and gorge below. The riverbed is generally dry.

> **Minerve** was the site of a mass execution of Cathars in the 13th century. Simon de Montfort laid siege to the town in June 1211, when 200 soldiers defended it under the generalship of Count Guilhem of Minerve. The crusaders used four stone-throwing machines to wreak terrible destruction, and eventually they cut off the defenders' water supply. After five weeks' siege the town sought to negotiate a surrender. Arnaud-Amaury, the papal legate, proposed that the townspeople be let free if they renounced the Cathar faith. He did this in the knowledge that few would accept the offer; 140 Cathars refused to convert and were burnt at the stake on the banks of the Cesse. De Montfort then razed the castle.
>
> Follow the road as it climbs to the top of the village. The streets are narrow and lined with stone-built houses, and packed with tourists at holiday times. There is a tower at the western entrance and a church at the centre, and a few restaurants and shops. Wine can be bought direct from producers operating an outlet near the church.
>
> A narrow path leads from the village to the bottom of the gorge, from where a large cavern can be seen under the mountain; it is possible to walk through this to a clearing on the other side. You can't cycle here and will need to lock and leave your bike should you want to explore the riverbed.

It's a further 4km east to La Caunette, the next village on this trip. Recross the bridge over the gorge and turn left onto the D10. Cycle with the gorge on your left and the mountains on your right. This road undulates and may be busy in summer.

Enter **La Caunette** by turning left onto a long narrow bridge. Continue on the Rue de l'Ormeau, passing a small church at the village's edge.

*CYCLING THE CANAL DU MIDI*

> The nave of Notre Dame de l'Assomption in **La Caunette** dates from the 11th century, while the remainder dates from the 16th century. The village is small and picturesque with a medieval centre, entered through a gate in a 13th-century tower. The old centre is worth exploring with tiny streets and lanes and wonderful examples of local architecture. Good wines are produced here; one producer's premises are beside the village gate, and you can smell the wine as you pass by.

Leave the village by following the road east to a roundabout. Take the D177, following a signpost for Aigues-Vives. At the crossroads turn right and cross the bridge onto the D907, travelling east in the direction of Aigues-Vives, Olonzac. Reach a right turn approximately

*Curved street in Aigne*

## EXCURSION – FROM HOMPS TO MINERVE

1km later, with a sign for Aigne, Olonzac. Take this road, the D177, to Aigne 1km further along.

At a T-junction in **Aigne** turn right onto the D910 in the direction of Beaufort, Olonzac.

> **Aigne**'s unusual old centre, known as l'Escargot (the snail), is laid out in a spiral shape around the church, St Martin – an ancient village layout. The old part of the village is on your left as you cycle on the Beaufort road approximately 50m from the T-junction. It's easy to miss as it is set back from the road. Enter the spiral through an old arch with a coat of arms above it. The arch is unusual as the streets on either side open from it directly. Straight ahead leads to the small square where you'll find the church; left or right will bring you to the same point. The church dates from the 10th century. Artisans live in some of the houses and you'll see examples of their work around the old village and beside the church.

Continue downhill towards **Beaufort** 5.5km away. As its name implies, the central point of this village is the large fort on the hill. The church on the right-hand side has an apse dating from Roman times and a door from the time of Emperor Charlemagne. Wander around the outside of the fort to see its ramparts.

There is a crossroads under the fort. Take the left turn on the D168 up a steep hill beside the fort. This is the road to Oupia which, being less than 2km away, becomes visible very quickly. There is an excellent view of Beaufort from the road.

**Oupia** retains some of its ancient fortifications and gates around the village. There is a small working château on the southwest of the town and a small shop in its centre. Leave the town by the D52E2 following the sign for Olonzac, with a wonderful view of Beaufort on the right. Olonzac is reached after 5km, and Homps regained via the outward route.

*CYCLING THE CANAL DU MIDI*

# STAGE 4
*Homps to Béziers*

| | |
|---|---|
| **Distance** | 63km excluding detours and excursion |
| **Path** | Generally good: bad patches, particularly near Pigasse bridge and after Argeliers; roots and occasional subsidence between Malpas Tunnel and nine locks at Béziers |
| **Shade** | Good, but some patches with limited or no shade |
| **Descent** | 20m |
| **Map** | 72 or 65 IGN *Carte de Promenade* |
| **Detours** | To Argens-Minervois, Ventenac-en-Minervois, Capestang, Colombiers and Béziers; Oppidum d'Ensérune |
| **Excursion** | From Canal de Junction and Canal de la Robine to Narbonne and Port la Nouvelle (74km) |

This stage passes through or close to small Minervois villages such as Argens-Minervois or Venentac-en-Minervois. Mountain ranges can be spotted to north and south while cycling along a 54km-lock-free stretch of waterway. The canal to Narbonne and Port la Nouvelle branches off this stage. You pass the medieval town of Capestang, the drained Montady lake, Malpas Tunnel, the ancient ruins at Ensérune, finishing at Béziers' nine locks – one of the wonders of the Canal du Midi.

### Leaving Homps port
Follow the path on the south side. The path is good to **Homps lock**, a single lock with a picnic spot on the north side, approximately 1km away. Continue to double-chambered **Ognon lock** 700m later, with a restaurant close by. There is a mill race beside the lock; cross the River Ognon here too. Approximately 200m later you come to a road and path; stick with the towpath but watch out for tree roots. Within 2km reach **Pechlaurier**

## STAGE 4 – HOMPS TO BÉZIERS

**Stage 4: Homps to Béziers**

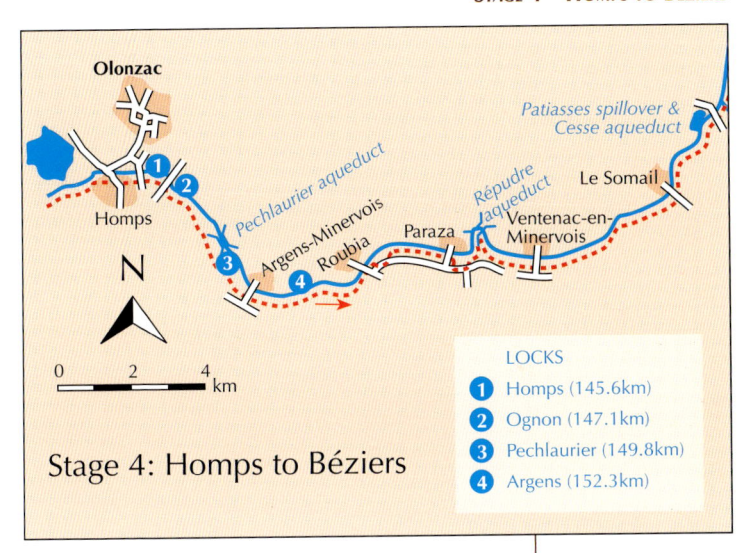

**LOCKS**
1. Homps (145.6km)
2. Ognon (147.1km)
3. Pechlaurier (149.8km)
4. Argens (152.3km)

aqueduct and then two-chambered **Pechlaurier lock**. Immediately after this pass an escarpment that separates the canal from the River Aude.

The two-towered château of **Argens-Minervois** dominates the right bank of the canal as you pedal on from Pechlaurier lock. Perched on high, it overshadows the village of that name.

map continues on pages 110–11

### DETOUR TO ARGENS-MINERVOIS

Cross a bridge to the north side to visit **Argens-Minervois**; a modern port, Port Occitainie, sits beside the bridge on the northern bank. Note a cemetery on your left as you cycle into the village. Close to this and near the canal are the ruins of a 10th-century church, of which only a few arches and a wall remain. The 14th-century château is impressive and appears in good repair. The road leads straight up to its ramparts. Argens has the dubious distinction of having been, in 1356, sold to pay a ransom for the release of John the Good who was a prisoner of the English forces.

Return to the canal by the same route.

*Argens-Minervois château and town*

Continue along the south side of the canal on the towpath in a easterly direction towards **Argens lock**. This highly significant lock is approximately 1km from the village. It lies 32m above sea level, and the cycle route maintains this level for the next 54km. The next lock encountered is the first of a stairway of eight outside Béziers.

The path is wide and gravelly here. Look out for Montrabech Tower to the south shortly after passing the lock, the remains of a 12th-century château. The current château produces well-regarded Corbières wines. Note small kilometre markings on the edge of the path, measuring the distance from the lock, which eventually peter out.

From Argens lock onwards a series of small villages and towns is passed. This stretch is especially pleasant as you pedal from the Minerve into the Corbières region. **Roubia** is reached 2.5km after the lock, a pleasant little village accessed across the canal bridge. You must cycle on the road alongside the canal (D124) for a short distance outside Roubia; this road may be busy so exercise care. The next town is **Paraza**.

## STAGE 4 – HOMPS TO BÉZIERS

Pierre Paul Riquet lodged in **Paraza** in 1620, and his son also stayed here during the canal's construction. The town has attractive streets lined with long-established businesses and old houses. The château is at the top of the town, and there is an excellent view over the plain from the upper part of the town.

Return to the D124 for a short distance and then rejoin the towpath. This is marked *la balade de riquet* (Riquet's walk). **Répudre aqueduct** is found approximately 1km after Paraza, and is the second-oldest canal bridge in the world. Riquet devised it and Vauban used it as the template for many more. Scramble down the bank beside the aqueduct for a glimpse of the arch and a plaque above it commemorating Riquet's work. Your view may be partially obscured by bamboo plants.

*Répudre aqueduct*

## CYCLING THE CANAL DU MIDI

*Ventenac-en-Minervois*

### DETOUR TO VENTENAC-EN-MINERVOIS

The village of **Ventenac-en-Minervois** is 2km from the aqueduct on the northern side. The old château is built around a tower visible from the canal; the château's wine outlet faces directly onto the canal and sells a range of Minervois wines. There is a pleasant restaurant/café on the road leading to the village, where the chef cooks meat over an open fire in full view of the customers.

Return to the canal by the same route.

Continue on the road on the south side for approximately 1.4km. Note the towpath to the left as the road bears away from the canal. The path is wide, good and with a gravelly surface. Note a path to the right approximately 1.5km along the towpath signed for St-Nazaire d'Aude, a village visible from the path. Shortly afterwards, a small bridge crosses over a tributary on the northern bank of the canal. A further 0.5km on reach an elegant striated stone bridge. Pass under it to join a road that leads towards Le Somail.

## STAGE 4 – HOMPS TO BÉZIERS

**Le Somail** is a 17th-century village built to support canal traffic. It has a small port with a narrow cobbled bridge linking the two banks. There are restaurants and *chambres d'hôtes* on both sides, making this a good stopping point. The village possesses two interesting features: a museum of hats and headwear (close to 7000 exhibits), and a second-hand and antique bookshop with a stock of over 50,000 volumes. There is also a small tower and church on the northern bank.

The next few kilometres bring a series of important canal works and landmarks: l'Epanchoir des Patiasses, the Minervoises ports, the River Cesse crossing, the junction with the canal system that leads to Narbonne and ultimately the Mediterranean Sea, and the Maison des Patiases.

Pass a wooden sign for the Hotel/Restaurant Domaine du Somail on your right when leaving Le Somail. The small holiday complex has a swimming pool, restaurant and rooms in chalet-style bungalows in its grounds.

The first construction encountered after Le Somail is the **Epanchoir des Patiasses** (spillover), which helps regulate the water levels in the canal. It is a large vertical barrier with six openings, an overflow system which was built in 1694. Look out for the torrents of water underneath as you cross the works.

*Épanchoir des Patiasses*

*Cycling the Canal du Midi*

Maison des Patiasses is a *chambre d'hôte* beside the works of the same name, with a restaurant and space for those wishing to camp in the garden at its rear.

Almost immediately after the crossing the Ports of Minervois come into view on the northern bank, where moored canal boats enjoy shade from overhanging trees. Since a detour is necessary to reach these it's probably best to observe them from the towpath.

The crossing of the Cesse river is dramatic, particularly in winter when the river is in flood. The bridge carrying the canal was built between 1689 and 1690 and significantly repaired in the mid-19th century; it is 64m long and 20m above the river. Take one of the paths on either side of the bridge to get a better view of the arches. The towpath is wide and cobbled on the bridge

## Stage 4: Homps to Béziers (continued)

**LOCKS**
5. Fonsérannes (206.5km)

*Quarante aqueduct*
*Canal du Midi*
Argeliers
Junction of two canal systems (168.6km)
*Canal de Jonction*
Patiasses spillover & Cesse aqueduct
*Répudre aqueduct*
Le Somail
Paraza  Ventenac-en-Minervois

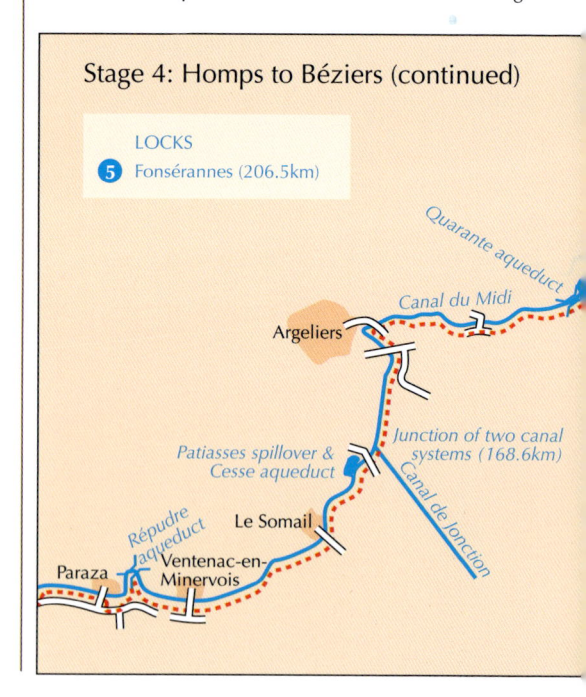

map continued from page 105

## STAGE 4 – HOMPS TO BÉZIERS

itself. There are boats moored semi-permanently on the opposite bank; these may include an old Amsterdam barge, *de Drje Gebroeders,* built in 1894. It often has its mast raised and a small sail unfurled.

The junction with the **Canal de Jonction** is reached shortly after crossing the Cesse river. The Canal de Jonction is the first part of the canal and river system that leads to Narbonne and from there to Port la Nouvelle and the Mediterranean Sea. ▶

Cross the footbridge to continue on the Canal du Midi towpath. Watch out for hens scratching around in front of the cottage beside the bridge. A factory on the northern bank of the canal spoils the view somewhat. A lovely row of pine trees shades the path, and in summer the air is heavily scented. Cycle through a cutting for

For details of an excursion along the Canal de Junction and Canal de la Robine to Narbonne and Port la Nouvelle, see the end of Stage 4.

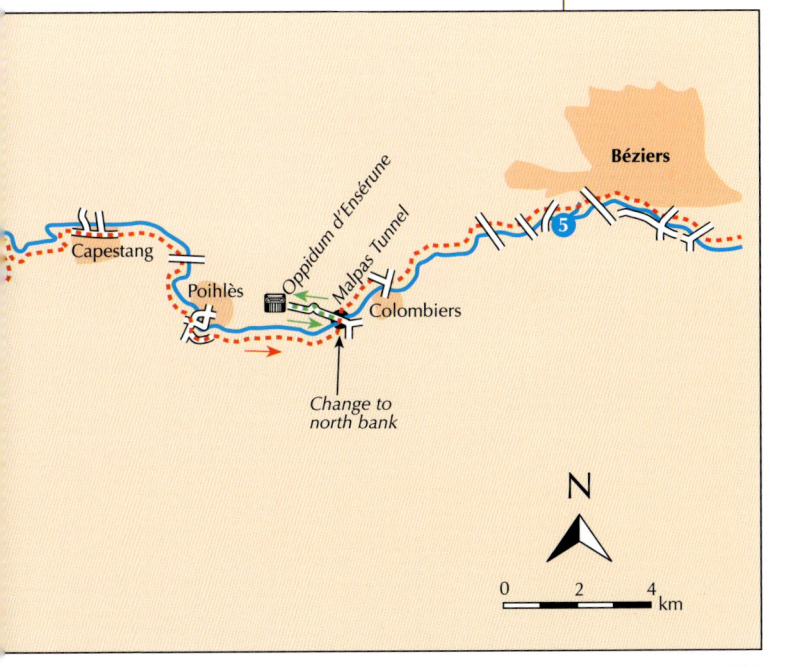

2km until a road is reached. The towpath is very narrow with exposed tree roots; it is easier to stay on the road until you reach the bridge that can be seen ahead.

Cross a busy road, then rejoin the path. There is a choice between an upper and lower path; the upper path gives a better view of the town of **Argeliers**. Continue to the next bridge, also the location of Argeliers port. There is a restaurant, le Chat Qui Peche ('the cat who fishes') on the canal's northern bank. The original house was built by Riquet.

Continue on the path for the next 5km to a bridge, Pont de Pigasse, built in 1684. It may be necessary to climb up to the road and then descend on the other side as the path under the bridge floods, or may be too mucky to cycle safely. The road to the north leads to the village of Cruzy, 5km away. At the next bridge cross a road before the Relais de Pigasse, a restaurant and wine seller offering wine tasting. The original *relais* was a stopping place for those travelling the canal in passenger barges.

The path narrows after the *relais* and is mucky, with some subsidence: take care. The **Quarante aqueduct** is reached after 1km. This three-arched aqueduct, constructed between 1693 and 1727, crosses over the River Quarante. The church at Capestang comes into view

*View of the drained Montady lake*

## STAGE 4 – HOMPS TO BÉZIERS

3km after the aqueduct. The canal meanders at this stage, and takes a further 3km to reach the port at Capestang.

Capestang port is situated between two bridges to the north of the town and is well shaded, particularly on the southern side. The road to the north of the port leads to the town of Puisserguier. There is an aqueduct, du Saisses, close to the port, which channels the water from the Saisses. There was a devastating flood in 1766 when part of the canal collapsed and released a torrent of water that destroyed much of the town. There are picnic tables close to the aqueduct.

### DETOUR TO CAPESTANG

**Capestang** was a prosperous town in the Middle Ages, gaining much of its wealth from salt harvested from Capestang lake (now drained). The town's enormous church, visible from the canal, is the Collegiate St-Etienne dating from the 13th century, and once the secondary residence of the Archbishop of Narbonne. However, the fortified building remains unfinished. The church is open for one hour out of season (9–10am) and 9am–12pm and 4–7pm on Sundays and Fridays in season. The town has narrow streets leading to an attractive main square. There are a restaurants, shops and general services.

Leave Capestang, still on the south bank, and pass over the Epanchoir de Pietat. This overflow was built after the 1766 catastrophe. Approximately 3km from Capestang pass some exercise bars and public fitness installations. There are boats moored along this part of the canal, making it an informal port.

There are very good views of the drained **Montady lake**, and its radial design is visible (best seen from the Oppidum d'Ensérune, below). The local lords of the area surrounding Montady decided to drain the lake in 1247, and used a series of radial ditches to carry the water to a central drain over 1.3km long that passes under the Ensérune.

## Cycling the Canal du Midi

*Barge offering chambres d'hôtes at Poilhès*

**Poilhès** is a pleasant village 5.5km from Capestang. Cross a modern overflow system as you enter the town, and pass a barge, the *Alegria*, now converted for bed and breakfast accommodation. The path brings you into the village centre. Note an attractive building with a clock tower on the northern bank. As it passes through the village, the towpath merges with the old Roman road, the *Via Domitia*, for a short period. Poilhès takes its name from the Latin *Podium Valerii*. There are two antique English cannons on the right-hand side of the path as you leave the village.

Reach an old bridge 2km beyond Poilhès; look out for the **Oppidum d'Ensérune** on the hill on the northern

*Malpas Tunnel*

## STAGE 4 – HOMPS TO BÉZIERS

> **Malpas Tunnel** is one of major works on the canal: 170m long, 7m high and 8m wide, and one of Riquet's great achievements. He began work on it in 1679 against the advice of the king's local attendant. Riquet realised that he had to act quickly and completed the tunnelling in eight days, just before the formal order stopping the works arrived.
>
> The tunnel was the first of its kind built for a canal, and is unique in other ways too. It represents a junction of three modes of transport and a major drainage system. There is a road on top; below that is the canal; below that again is the tunnel, dug in 1855, carrying the Bordeaux to Sète railway line; finally, underneath everything, is the drain that carries away the water from Montady lake.

side of the canal. The Malpas Tunnel is reached 2km later. It is not possible to cycle through the tunnel but there is a walkway for pedestrians on the northern side. Climb to the road to find the tourist office across the road and slightly to the right. **You must cross to the northern bank of the canal at this point.** ▶ A path continues on the southern side but it leads away from the canal. Descend to the pedestrian walkway using a flight of steps on the northern side. Lock your bike securely as it will be out of view while you are underground.

*Change to the north side.*

There are picnic tables and plenty of places to stop and rest. The tourist office gives information about the locality, and has local produce for sale.

### DETOUR TO OPPIDUM D'ENSÉRUNE

This detour gives an insight into pre-Roman civilisation – dating back to the Iron Age – and involves a climb to 120m above sea level (the only high ground in the area). The site of the **Oppidum d'Ensérune** is approximately 2km from the canal at the Malpas Tunnel. Take the small road that crosses the tunnel and follow the sign for the Oppidum, cycling northwards. ▶

*Remains of houses with sunken urns at Oppidum d'Ensérune*

◀ The road climbs steeply and twists and turns to reach the entrance. There is an excellent view of the drained Montady lake as you climb through the pine wood. Although this is a short cycle, the climb feels steep and can be hot in summer.

The ruins of this ancient fortified town are perched on top of a steep hill and have a commanding view of the surrounding villages and countryside. You can walk round the site and visit a museum displaying artefacts from the different periods of occupation.

There are remains suggesting that people settled on the hilltop as far back as the 6th century BC, during the first Iron Age. Little evidence of these first settlers remains except for some food stores dug into the rock. The second occupation dates from the 5th to the end of the 3rd centuries BC. The settlers built a proper town with stone houses, streets and defensive ramparts. Each house had pottery jars sunk into the floor to store food. There was a burial ground to the west of and separated from the main town. The town was prosperous, and there is evidence of significant trade with Greece and Rome. The architecture from that period reflects outside influences. The houses were larger and built around a central courtyard; columns echo Greek and Roman design. ▶

## STAGE 4 – HOMPS TO BÉZIERS

◀ The site was abandoned in the 3rd century BC; it is possible that Hannibal destroyed it as he led his army to Rome. The Romans settled the hill in the last century BC. The site was abandoned in the 1st century AD when the introduction of *Pax Romana* led to safer living conditions on the plain.

Grain silos sunk into the ground can be seen on the hill. The town was significant – the site today measures 600m from east to west and 150m from north to south. Apart from the archaeological interest, the views are tremendous. On a clear day Canigou mountain in the Pyrenees can be seen to the south, the Cevennes mountains to the north, the drained Montady lake, the line of the *Via Domitia*, and the Canal du Midi.

The museum is housed in a villa built in 1915 and converted for its present purpose in 1937. The ground floor is devoted to finds from the settlements, organised both by chronology and theme. The first floor displays the artefacts from the cremation burial site. The museum is due to undergo refurbishment in the next few years.

Return to the **northern bank of the canal** and pedal towards Colombiers. The path is clay but good and well shaded. **Colombiers** is reached after 2km. The old hump-backed bridge dates from Riquet's time; close by are two washhouses. Adults play *petanque* (boules) just beside the bridge on the northern side, and children dive into the canal from the bridge in the summer heat.

### DETOUR TO COLOMBIERS

**Colombiers** is lovely and well worth a quick visit. The church of St Sylvestre was rebuilt in the 19th century but preserves some of its earlier architectural features. It is built on the same site as two earlier churches, thus entitling the residents to describe the town as 'Colombiers of the three churches'. There is a modern port with a restaurant and other services, and the château on the southern bank also has a restaurant. A private clinic doubles as a bed and breakfast – you stay in one of the private rooms.

Cross the road at the old bridge and continue towards Béziers on the northern bank. There is a choice of paths at this stage: upper and lower. The upper one gives great views of Montady – identified by its 12th-century tower – and mountains in the distance. The path drops steeply after 2.5km; take care at this point. It is possible to continue on the upper path until it meets a road in less than 1km; then join the towpath.

There are exposed roots on this stretch, some marked with red or blue paint. Pass under three road bridges, the first of which is approximately 3km after Colombiers. Be careful of the deep puddles, especially in bad weather. The path is narrow; take care when passing other towpath users.

There are good views of Béziers as you approach the **Fonsérannes locks**. These 'nine' locks are the most dramatic works on the canal system, and enable the canal to drop 22m and join the Orb river. Boats crossed the river and then re-joined the canal. An aqueduct, built in 1855, obviated the need for the river crossing.

> **Fonsérannes locks** form a water staircase for barges. It is well worth stopping and watching boats ascend and descend. The locks operate in the morning and afternoon with a break between 12pm and 2pm. There is a mechanical lifting system on the southern bank of the canal. The buildings on each side of the canal originally housed canal workers; there is also a restaurant and a church. Although still referred to as the 'nine' locks, there are only eight locks now. In addition, the seventh lock is a basin that leads to the aqueduct that crosses the Orb. The eighth lock is no longer used as it leads to a branch of the canal that served Béziers.

There is a variety of routes into **Béziers** proper. Those wishing to stick to the canal paths should cross the branch canal using the footbridge at the final lock (closest to Béziers and after the Canal du Midi bears to the right). Cycle along the track until a road is reached. Cross this and continue along the Chemin du Quai du Porte Notre Dame. Turn left at the next road (800m from

*Stage 4 – Homps to Béziers*

*View of the locks at Fonsérannes*

Fonsérannes), and turn right at the next junction. The road is busy from here to the centre. Approach a bridge (Pont Neuf, or new bridge) and cross the Orb river, from which there is an excellent view of the old bridge upriver.

Follow the road through the traffic lights and climb the hill to a roundabout; keep straight ahead. Note an entrance into an underground car park on your left, with a ramped path beside it; dismount and wheel your bike up this to reach Place Jean Jaurès (Jean Jaurès Square). Alternatively, continue on the road to reach the roundabout at the top of the Plateau des Poètes (Poets' Park) in the centre of Béziers.

### Béziers

Béziers is the birthplace of Pierre Paul Riquet, who is honoured with an imposing statue in the centre of the town's main thoroughfare, Allées Paul Riquet. This tree-lined pedestrianised space stretches from the Plateau des Poètes to the municipal theatre, and is the location for markets, festivals, concerts, parades and a range of other outdoor communal activities.

*Béziers*

The town boasts 7000 years of history and a vibrant present. The Iberian Celts were the first people to inhabit the site in any numbers (8th century BC), and the town was taken over by the Greeks two centuries later. The Greeks traded all around the world and there is evidence of commercial links with Asia, North Africa and the Eastern Mediterranean.

The Romans took the town in 121BC, and set about reorganising it. They built the old bridge across the Orb, and established Béziers as the regional centre for viniculture. St Aphrodise (who arrived in town on a camel – the animal is celebrated annually) was beheaded by the local townsfolk – and subsequently coverted the town to Christianity.

Béziers' worst day was undoubtedly 22 July 1209, when crusaders massacred its 20,000 inhabitants (see Introduction). Not surprisingly, the town sank into relative obscurity. Gradually its fortunes revived until the 19th-century renaissance when it reaped the financial benefits of the wine trade. A change in the fortunes of

## STAGE 4 – HOMPS TO BÉZIERS

that trade at the beginning of the 20th century brought Béziers to international attention again. Between 1904 and 1907 winegrowers and those working in the industry became concerned at the drop in the price that they received for their wine. The focus of their frustration was those wholesalers who watered down wine or used excessive quantities of sugar to increase the quantity produced (see Introduction).

Béziers has one further claim to fame: as the birthplace of Jean Moulin, one of the heroes of the French Resistance during World War II. Moulin reorganised, reinvigorated and led his colleagues until he was arrested, tortured and killed in June 1943.

Béziers is an easy town to visit. Its main attractions are situated close together, and are easy to reach on a bike. The arena (bullring) is the most distant place of interest, just 1km from the main square. The central square and **Allées Paul Riquet** give a good sense of the entire town. The municipal theatre (1844) is at the top of the Allées; refurbished by the local authority in the early part of this century, its wooden interior is considered to be an especially good example of such an architectural style. Plays, operas, concerts and variety shows are staged throughout the year.

**St-Nazaire Cathedral** is the town's main attraction. It dominates the skyline and is the most visible feature on the cycle from Colombiers. It is positioned on a small terrace, the **Place des Albigeois**, overlooking the River Orb, and has spectacular views over the river and surrounding countryside. The cathedral is entered through a side door on the square. There is an interesting carving of a beheading over the door, which represents the martyrdom of St Nazaire. Inside the cathedral is tall and airy; worth noting are the choir and the organ, as well as the side chapels and altars.

The 14th-century cloisters are beside the cathedral, and access is gained through a small doorway. Down a small flight of steps beside and below the cloisters is a wonderful terraced garden (**Jardin des Évêques**), thought to be on the site of one of the original settlements.

**Place des Bon Amis** (Square of the Good Friends) is close to the cathedral, and records an unsuccessful revolt against the Duke of Berry, when four of the opposing leaders were beheaded. The sculpture on the corner of the square (marked with a plaque) represents the now barely discernible heads of the unfortunate rebels. The **Place St-Cyr** continues the same theme, where there is a replica of a sculpture showing the decapitated St Aphrodise holding his head before him.

Those interested in churches will find plenty of interest in Béziers. Apart from the cathedral, there is **St Madeleine church**, scene of the murder of Viscount Trencavel in 1167 and the massacre of thousands during the sacking of the town in 1209. The church of the **Blue Penitents** has an unusual representation of women saints on the Provencal coast. **St Aphrodise** church has an elaborate Gothic altar with marble pillars, and faded (but interesting) murals.

The town's covered markets are worth a look, and are a good source of fresh provisions in the morning. The market (**Les Halles**), on Rue P. Riquet, is built on the site of a paupers' graveyard which was once attached to the now-demolished church of St Felix. The museum of fine art is located near the cathedral and has an excellent collection of work by local artists. The Bitterois museum houses a collection of archaeological finds from the Gallo-Roman period onwards and is in the former barracks, St-Jacques (Avenue de la Marne).

Evidence of Roman Béziers can be found in the old Roman arena (Rue des Anciennes Arenes). There are few actual Roman remains but the shape of the amphitheatre can still be discerned. The modern arena is a little further from the centre of the town. Bull-fighting is popular in the region and fights are staged in the arena (**Avenue St-Saëns**), as well as open-air concerts and operas in the summer.

The tourist office is on **Avenue St-Saëns**. Béziers is well known for its festivals, including its **Festa d'Oc** and *feria* in summer and its wine festival in autumn.

*Stage 4 – Homps to Béziers*

*St Madeleine church*

*Cycling the Canal du Midi*

## EXCURSION
### to Narbonne and Port la Nouvelle

| | |
|---|---|
| **Distance** | 74km |
| **Path** | Good, except crossing the Aude (on a little-used railway bridge); longer road alternative |
| **Shade** | Good on path to Narbonne; very exposed from Narbonne to Port la Nouvelle |
| **Descent** | 32m |
| **Map** | 72 IGN *Carte de Promenade* |

The Narbonne canal network is an important element in the Canal du Midi system. Two canals make up this system: Jonction and de la Robine. The latter was the first constructed (1686), and connects the Aude river to Narbonne and from there to the sea. Merchants transfered goods by cart from the Canal du Midi to the Canal de la Robine for over 100 years until the Canal de Jonction was finally built.

The stretch of canal from Narbonne is strikingly different from the rest of the system. It is very exposed and runs between two lagoons, Etang de Bages et de Sigean and Etang de l'Ayrolle, on a narrow strip of land shared with the railway line.

From the Canal du Midi take the right-hand path (western side) along the edge of the straight and 5km-long **Canal de Jonction**. The path is good quality and joins the road as it descends towards the village of **Sallèles d'Aude**. During the first 4km a series of six single locks is passed: **Cesse**, **Truilhas**, **Empare**, **Argeliers**, **St-Cyr** and **Sallèles**.

Just after Argeliers lock note a signpost for Amphoralis, a museum of ancient pottery and an archaeological site on the east side of the canal. It has a working kiln built with identical tools and materials to those used in Gallo-Roman times. **Sallèles-d'Aude** is a small village mainly on the western bank of the Canal de

## Excursion – to Narbonne and Port la Nouvelle

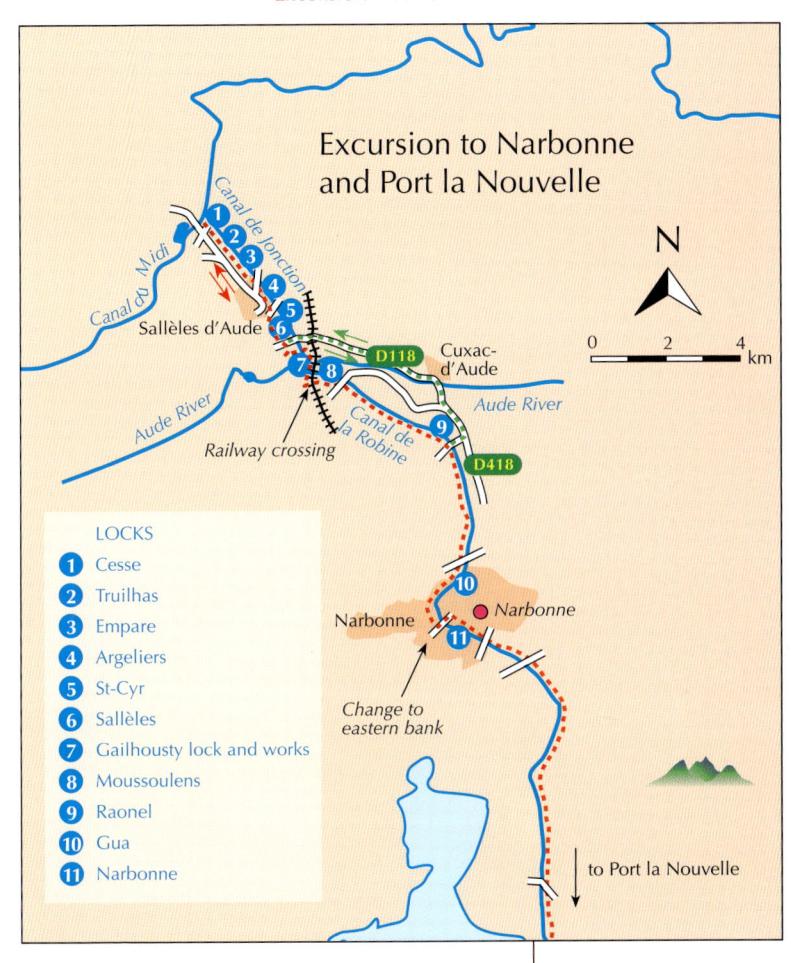

### Excursion to Narbonne and Port la Nouvelle

**LOCKS**
1. Cesse
2. Truilhas
3. Empare
4. Argeliers
5. St-Cyr
6. Sallèles
7. Gailhousty lock and works
8. Moussoulens
9. Raonel
10. Gua
11. Narbonne

Jonction and has been occupied continuously since pre-historic times. It became a centre for pottery production in the first 300 years of the 1st millennium. Apart from the Amphoralis museum the village has also a museum displaying traditional crafts and tools.

map continues on page 133

*Cycling the Canal du Midi*

The works at **Gailhousty** can be seen clearly from the bridge at Sallèles-d'Aude and are among the most significant on the canal network, accessed by a 1km cycle along the western side of the canal. The works include a double lock and an overflow system, the latter built in 1780 to drain Capestang lagoon. Unfortunately, the French Revolution interrupted this work and it was never fully completed. The overflow has 16 sluice gates under the main housing structure. Devastating floods in December 1999 damaged the works, and at the time of writing these are being restored. They are still worth visiting even if shrouded in scaffolding.

The canal joins the Aude river for approximately 50m at this point. Boats leave the Canal de Jonction through the Gailhousty lock, cross the Aude and join the **Canal de la Robine** at **Moussoulens lock**.

*Barge passing through Gailhousty*

## EXCURSION – TO NARBONNE AND PORT LA NOUVELLE

To follow the canal it is necessary to cross the Aude river. Cross to the eastern side of the canal using a footbridge at Gailhousty lock, then pass behind the main building and over the sluices. Note a small clay path on the left-hand side of the main path, marked by a waystone. Climb here to a railway line to find a metal bridge ahead (see photographs).

Cross the Aude using the railway bridge. Note that a tourist train uses this line occasionally and **you must take care when using this bridge**. The train travels slowly but check that the line is clear and that you can cross it quickly. Dismount when crossing.

Descend to the west bank of the river by means of a very steep path on the right at the end of the bridge, with a wonderful view of the Aude. Note a wide weir on your left. Pass under the bridge and re-join the canal towpath rising up to Moussoulens lock just 50m away. This lock is an important defence against the Aude floods.

**Above left:**
*The point where the path branches to go to the railway bridge*

**Above right:**
*Railway bridge crossing*

**Note** Those not wishing to use the railway bridge should return to Sallèles-d'Aude. Cross the road bridge in the village and follow the D118 to **Cuxac-d'Aude** 5km away. This road runs alongside the Aude river. In Cuxac take a right turn at the junction with the D418, direction Narbonne, and re-join the canal at Raonel (see below). These roads are busy during the tourist season.

*Cycling the Canal du Midi*

From Moussoulens follow the towpath on the west side of the canal as far as **Raonel lock** 4km away. This path has good shade and is easy to cycle. There are few houses close by and plenty of small tracks leading into fields and vineyards.

Join the Itinéraire cyclable, **La Littorale** (cycle path) to **Gua lock** 4km away. There is a good view of Narbonne cathedral on the city's outskirts, and a ruined mill at Gua lock. Join the road on your right as you approach the lock buildings, which runs alongside allotments and skirts the lock buildings. Pass a retirement home on your right, bear left and re-join the canal at the quay. Continue along the quay to reach a footbridge. Wheel your bike across this to the eastern canal bank. ◄

> Change to eastern bank.

Make your way through Narbonne by cycling along the quay eventually to pass under Voltaire bridge, the third bridge after the railway bridge. You must join the road to pass Dillon Quay and continue to Pont de la Liberté (Liberté bridge). Cross the road here and join a marked cycle path – **still on the eastern side of the canal.**

### Narbonne

A real gem, Narbonne is a city with something to interest most tastes. Founded in 118BC by a Roman Senate decree, the town, originally named Colonia Narbo Martius, became strategically important for the Roman Empire: it was the crossroads between the *Via Domitia* and the *Via Aquitania*.

The *Via Domitia* linked Rome with the Iberian peninsula. Hannibal led his army (including his elephants) along this road on his way to invade Rome. The *Via Aquitania* branched from the *Via Domitia* at Narbonne; the *Aquitania* went to Toulouse and eventually to the Atlantic at Bordeaux. Part of the original *Via Domitia* is preserved in the centre of the city's main square, **Place de l'Hôtel de Ville**.

The city changed hands over the following centuries with first the Visigoths, then the Arabs and eventually Pépin the Short taking it. It had a harbour and there are

## EXCURSION – TO NARBONNE AND PORT LA NOUVELLE

records of large ships using its port until the 14th century. Gradually the Aude estuary silted up, cutting the city off from the sea and creating a network of marshes and lagoons.

Charles Trénet (1913–2001) was one of Narbonne's most famous sons. The singer/songwriter gained international fame for his songs such as 'La Mer' ('Somewhere Beyond the Sea') 'Boum' and 'Qui reste-t-il de nos amours' (translated as 'I Wish You Love'). Trénet was an artist, poet and novelist as well as a musician. His songs are, in the main part, light and address quirky, nostalgic themes. His early life in Narbonne inspired many of his songs and he constantly referred to his native town and the surrounding countryside. The house where he was born now houses a small museum (13 Avenue Charles Trénet) displaying early drafts of his songs, and artefacts from his early life. A giant mural of Trénet, advertising the museum, can be seen close to the railway tracks to the west of the canal as you enter the city.

*Canal de la Robine passing through Narbonne*

*Sts Just and Saveur cathedral in Narbonne*

The cathedral of **Sts Just and Saveur** – never completely finished – dominates the skyline and dates from the 13th century. The cathedral's exterior is its most striking feature, and is dominated by buttresses and gargoyles. The interior is bathed with coloured light coming from tall, narrow, stained glass windows. The square cloisters are on the southern side of the cathedral; the **Jardin des Archevêques** (Archbishops' garden) is beside the cloisters and give a good view of the cathedral's exterior. The **Palais des Archevêques** (Archbishops' palace) is also beside the cathedral and houses a museum with a collection of Roman artefacts. It also has the second-largest collection of religious objects in France.

The **Donjon Gilles-Aycelin** is a fortified keep dating from the 13th century.

Narbonne has a daily covered market, and a large open-air market around the covered building on Sunday and Thursday mornings. The Sunday morning market is reputed to be one of the best in the region. The covered market is about 100m from the western bank of the canal close to the Liberté bridge.

Narbonne takes environmental issues seriously and promotes cycling both for its health and environmental benefits. It has a cycle-hiring scheme – you'll pass one of the cycle stands on the quays close to the Liberté bridge.

**From Narbonne to the sea**

> The path from Narbonne to Port la Nouvelle leads past lagoons, marshes and empty plains. You will rarely meet anyone on this stretch on the canal off-season, and note that there are no shops or services along the route.
>
> The path surface is clay, small stones and grit, and is easy to cycle. There are treeless stretches where you may be exposed to strong sunshine, even in winter. Make sure that you take sufficient water for the 22km cycle to the port as there are no places to refill along the way. The track is very exposed as you pass between the lagoons. The winds are frequent, strong and from all directions. Factor in extra time for your cycle when the wind is blowing or is forecast to strengthen.

Follow the east bank of the Canal de la Robine out of the city. The path is marked and weaves through car parks and public spaces along the canal's edge. Reach a gravel, hardened path on the city's outskirts. There is evidence of subsidence on the canal bank as you leave Narbonne, but it is still passable and repaired regularly. The canal skirts around a major retail zone in Narbonne suburbs, just before the path passes under the A9 autoroute. It has a hypermarket and a branch of sports goods chain, Decathlon. Note another canal branching off to the west as you leave the suburbs.

After 6.5km a cycle path branches off to the left of the towpath. This track goes to Gruissan (17.5km), Narbonne beach (14.5km) and St Pierre-sur-Mer (18km). On a clear day there should be views of the **Clape massif** (mountain range) on your left. The Clape region is well known for its wines.

After 8km **Mandirac lock**, with a large basin and curved sides, is reached. The road on your left leads to

*CYCLING THE CANAL DU MIDI*

*A fountain in Narbonne*

*Excursion – to Narbonne and Port la Nouvelle*

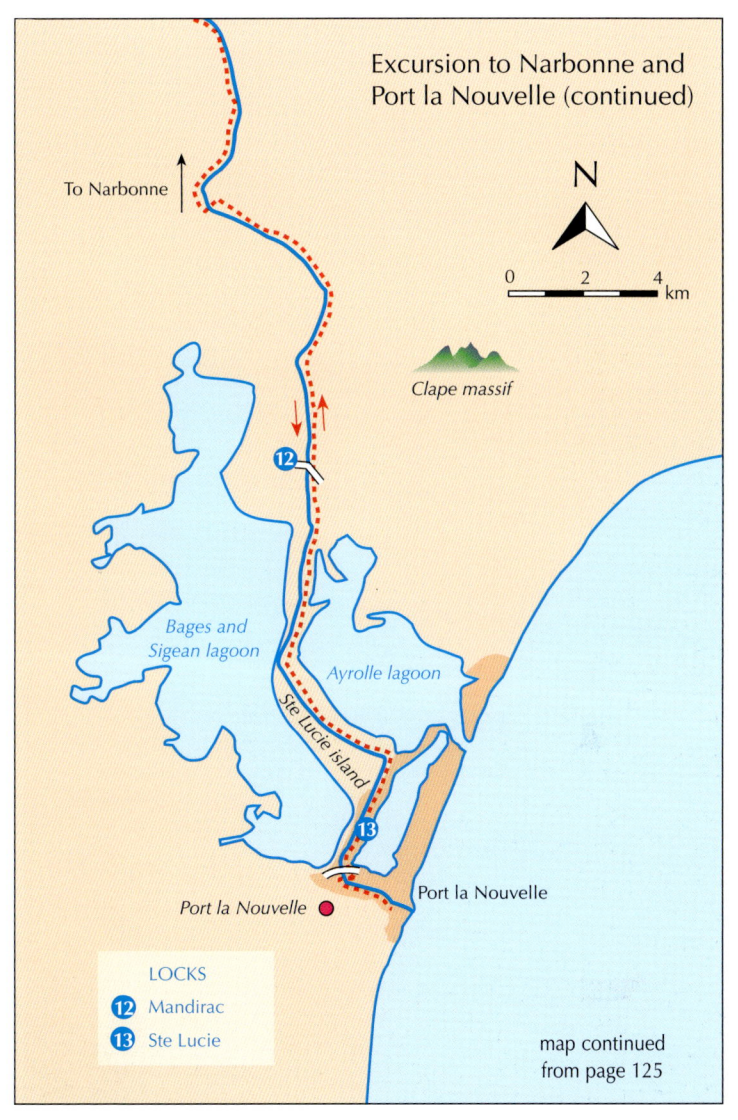

# Excursion to Narbonne and Port la Nouvelle (continued)

To Narbonne

N

0  2  4 km

Clape massif

Bages and Sigean lagoon

Ayrolle lagoon

Ste Lucie island

⑫

⑬

Port la Nouvelle

Port la Nouvelle

**LOCKS**
⑫ Mandirac
⑬ Ste Lucie

map continued from page 125

133

*Towpath leading to Port la Nouvelle*

the Clape massif and Gruissan. Within 2km the towpath passes close to the Campignol marsh and lagoon on the left and the **Bages and Sigean lagoon** on the right. **Campignol lagoon** gives way to **Ayrolle lagoon** and soon you are cycling between two large bodies of water. The canal shares this narrow strip of land with the railway track; the only sound heard will be that of the occasional train. Keep your eyes peeled for flocks of flamingos wading in the water.

Reach **Ste Lucie lock** 10km after Mandirac lock, on the island of Ste Lucie, a small nature reserve. Herbs grow wild here – there are identification tags on some of the bushes – and scent the air in warmer months. This is a lovely spot for picnicking or resting, and it is possible to cross to the other bank where you'll find more shade in a small wood.

## Excursion – to Narbonne and Port la Nouvelle

**Port la Nouvelle** is 3km from Ste Lucie island. The approach to the town is one of the least attractive on the canal system as it runs beside an oil storage depot. The towpath comes to a dead end at the quayside at the town's edge. Take the slip road that rises to a roundabout and cross the canal by bridge.

The town of **Port la Nouvelle** is a traditional seaside resort, with 13km of beaches and all the services and activities required for a beach holiday. It is also a busy fishing and commercial port with lots of trawlers and other craft. There are hotels and campsites in the town and surrounding area. Book in advance at peak holiday times – it's a long ride back to Narbonne.

Return to the Canal du Midi by the same route.

*Port la Nouvelle*

*CYCLING THE CANAL DU MIDI*

# Stage 5: Béziers to Sète

**LOCKS and PORTS**
1. Fonsérannes (206.5km)
2. Orb (208km)
3. Béziers port and lock (208.5km)
4. Ariège (212.5km)
5. Villeneuve-lès-Béziers (213.8km)
6. Portiragnes (218.3km)

map continues on pages 146–147

# STAGE 5
*Béziers to Sète*

| | |
|---|---|
| **Distance** | 43.5km excluding detours and excursions |
| **Path** | Tarmac to clay and stone |
| **Shade** | Moderate along canal; little between Agde and Sète |
| **Climb** | Flat; climbs on detours to Portiragnes water tower (20m) and Mont St Loup (144m) |
| **Maps** | 65 and 72 IGN *Carte de Promenade* |
| **Detours** | To Portiragnes water tower and village, Vias town and beach, Mont St-Loup and Marseillan |
| **Excursions** | From either the Fonsérannes locks or Villeneuve-lès-Béziers to Vendres salt lagoon (46 or 49km) Across Portiragnes marshes and to Séringnan (34km) |

This wonderful stage leads through Camargue-like marshes to Sète, the Venice of the Mediterranean, passing close to Portiragnes and Vias villages with their unique black-stone churches. You leave the canal at Agde, an ancient Greek port, then cycle beside a beautiful long sandy beach to reach the magical town of Sète.

### Leaving the Fonsérannes locks

Stay on the north side of the canal, but make sure to follow the Canal du Midi: it's easy to make a mistake here. Pass all the buildings and signs and you should see a barrier preventing cars from driving onto the towpath. There are two parking bays for people with disabilities, and a small footbridge nearby. Cross this and pass over the branch of the canal that leads to Béziers.

Once across the footbridge climb up the clay path that leads to the 240m-long **Orb aqueduct** which carries the canal over the Orb (Pont Canal de l'Orb). Built between 1854 and 1857, it was commissioned in 1858 and is popular with both townsfolk and tourists today.

## CYCLING THE CANAL DU MIDI

*View of the Orb and surrounding countryside from the cathedral in Béziers*

Stop as you cross to admire the view of Béziers and the Orb river 12m below. The towpath (north side) is cobbled and bumpy to ride.

The double-chambered **Orb lock** is at the end of the aqueduct, where the canal drops sharply. Take the path to the left, dropping steeply, then cycle around a barrier to the quay at **Béziers port**. Continue along the 200m quay, or on the road beside it, to the next double lock, **Béziers lock** (take the road to the left here should you wish to go to the railway station).

Pass behind the lock-keeper's house on the road side. Cross the road ahead and cycle on a gravelly lane, passing a turreted villa, Villa Vallespir, on the corner to your left. Pass an excellent restaurant, La Refinerie, on your left. There are tables outside in summer and it is a favourite lunchtime venue for local business people.

Change to the south bank.

**Cross to the south side** at the next bridge after the restaurant; this road is busy. ◄ There are two parallel bridges here, a road bridge and a wooden pedestrian

138

## STAGE 5 – BÉZIERS TO SÈTE

one. The latter is on the other side of the road and has one or two missing planks, but it is safe. Turn left onto the tarmac path as soon as you cross the bridge and before you reach the entrance to a sports stadium. A sign describes the cycle track and there is also a water tap (this is occasionally vandalised and cannot be relied upon). The path is a dedicated cycleway for almost all the 12km stretch to the second Portiragnes bridge. The towpath is beside the cycle path and runners and dog walkers may opt for that. Cyclists should stick to the tarmac track.

Cross a small road approximately 700m after joining the path, with a roundabout on one side. Continue on the cycle track. Watch out for a metal bridge 0.5km further on, a drawbridge that passes over the canal and allows containers to cross the canal, the towpath and then the road into a factory on the right. The bridge is above the canal most of the time, but is lowered when containers have to pass. Warning lights let you know when this is about to happen.

*Drawbridge between Béziers and Villeneuve-lès-Béziers*

*CYCLING THE CANAL DU MIDI*

For details of an excursion from either the Fonsérannes locks or Villeneuve-lès-Béziers to Vendres salt lagoon, see the end of Stage 5.

Look out for some small canalets as **Ariège lock** is approached. After the lock pass under a road bridge and then approach **Villeneuve-lès-Béziers**. The village and its distinctive church tower can be seen on the right as you cycle along the elevated track. The cycle track joins a road running alongside the canal for 100m as Villeneuve is entered. Note a small canal on your right. The **Villeneuve-lès-Béziers lock** is on the left-hand side; be careful here as you must cross a busy road at the bridge to rejoin the cycleway. ◄

> **Villeneuve-lès-Béziers** gets its name from the Latin *Villa Nova*, or new villa. The town has had a taxing history: the Frankish leader Charles Martel destroyed it in AD737, and it was sacked during the crusades, earning it the nickname *La Crémade* – the burnt place. There is a good pizza restaurant with the same name on the northern bank of the canal beside the bridge. St Etienne's church is the town's main feature. The church dates back to the 11th century but has undergone much modification since. The tower is unusual in that it is octagonal on a square base. There is a side chapel with a statue of St James, complete with cockleshell, indicating that the church was once on the pilgrimage route to Santiago de Compostella.
>
> The town has just renovated its main square and civic offices. The square is the location for open-air concerts held during a jazz festival, a country music festival, a *feria* and a Harley Davidson regional rally. The town has shops and other services including a hotel, bed and breakfasts and campsites.

Leave Villeneuve-lès-Béziers on the cycle track on the southern bank of the canal. There are barges permanently moored on both banks. Pass under a major road bridge before reaching a second old bridge. Note a village, **Cers**, in the distance on the northern side; this can be reached by crossing the bridge and following the road

*Stage 5 – Béziers to Sète*

as it passes over the main road. There is a small supermarket on the edge of the village.

Follow the cycle path to the next bridge, Pont de Caylus; take care when crossing this. Carry on the path to reach **Portiragnes lock**, 5km from Villeneuve.

### DETOUR TO PORTIRAGNES WATER TOWER AND VILAGE

**Portiragnes** water tower is perched on a hilltop (22.5m elevation) with an excellent view of the canal and countryside. Take the bridge to the north side of the canal. Cross the road and follow a small suburban street, Rue de la Pinède, climbing past some pine trees to reach the water tower. From here you can see the canal, Béziers, the village, Portiragnes marshes and the Mediterranean Sea.

Follow the road in front of the water tower towards the village (left when facing towards the canal). Turn right at the T-junction down Avenue du Général de Gaulle. ▶

*Portiragnes church and village from the water tower*

◀ Portiragnes is the first village on the trip where you encounter a church, St Felix's, built of black volcanic rock. The church dates from the 15th century and its black volcanic appearance is typical of the region. Such churches are known as the 'black churches', and you'll see them in towns and villages between Portiragnes and the Thau lagoon. The building stone comes from extinct volcanoes in the locality, such as Roque Haute, 2km to the east. Part of this is now a nature reserve open to visitors, and outdoor pursuits are available in season.

Portiragnes is the birthplace of a 12th-century woman troubadour, Azalaïs of Porcairagues. Today, the village is known for its *abrigado*, a form of bullrunning. Horse riders herd four or five young bulls through the main street, and the village men try to catch one of the bulls and wrestle it to a halt. Horsemen and women work as cattle herders on the ranches close to Portiragnes marsh and you can sometimes see them riding by, cowboy style.

The village has a small supermarket, bakers, and a newsagent, as well as restaurants and pizza outlets. The tourist office is in the village centre. One restaurant, Mon Rêve d'Enfant, opposite the Salle Polyvalente, is very popular and well worth visiting for lunch or an evening meal.

Portiragnes has two centres: Portiragnes village and **Portiragnes Plage** (beach). The village is lively all year around while the beach only comes to life in season when it is very busy. The beach is regularly awarded a European Blue Flag for the quality of its bathing waters.

Return to the canal by the same route.

Continue along the cycle track on the canal's south side. There is a water tap beside Portiragnes bridge. Cross a small bridge over a drainage channel, the Fossé du Nouu; a shaded area beside this is regularly used for picnics and rough camping. Once over the bridge cycle between the canal and Portiragnes marshes. These are flooded in winter, and the body of water is called the Estagnol, a favourite feeding and roosting spot for flocks of flamingos. You may also see black southern bulls and white Camargue horses in fields close to the path. This stretch of the canal and the drainage canals close by are home to otters and coypu, best seen in late evening or early morning.

## STAGE 5 – BÉZIERS TO SÈTE

Reach a road bridge 3km from Portiragnes lock. The cycle track turns to the right away from the canal, and leads to Portiragnes beach should you wish to spend some time swimming or relaxing. It is also the starting point for a short excursion across the marshes. ▶

Pass under the bridge that carries the road to Portiragnes Plage. This is a clay path which may be difficult to cycle in wet weather. There is a restaurant on your right. **Port Cassafières,** a base for the Crown Blue boat line, is reached after 800m; there is a restaurant here, and a barge offering bed and breakfast at the edge of the port. Circumvent the port following the path to a road, turn left, and left again to regain the towpath.

The **Libron works** are a further 3km along the canal. A series of gates regulate the Libron's flow so that in times of extreme flooding the river passes over the canal. These complex works were put in place in 1855 to deal with problems created by the fact that the canal and the

For details of an excursion across Portiragnes marshes and to Séringnan, see the end of Stage 5.

*Libron works*

*CYCLING THE CANAL DU MIDI*

river are below or close to sea level at this point, making it difficult to resolve the river crossing with an aqueduct.

The path continues on the south side to Agde but you can **change to the north side** at the Libron works as the path is better. ◄ Pass through a small gate to gain access to and across the works. This can be a bit difficult with a heavily laden bike. Dismount and climb up a steep bank to reach the path on the north side.

Change to the north bank.

There is a clear view of Vias church on your left and a funfair, Europark, on the southern bank. You can make detours to Vias town (1km north) or the beach (2.5km south) when you reach Vias port.

### DETOUR TO VIAS

**Vias** is first mentioned in official records in AD899. The fortified village was built in the 12th century. using local volcanic rock. The original village was circular with the church of St John the Baptist forming part of the defences; the bell tower was built as a watchtower. There is a beautiful rose window in the west wall of the church. The original window was destroyed when a nearby arms depot blew up in 1944, and the new one installed in 1955.

The locals have a special reverence for a statue of the Virgin Mary in the church's south chapel. Local legend claims that a ship crewed by Syrian sailors ran into a terrible storm. They promised to give the statue they had on board to the place where they found shelter– and that was Vias.

There is a small covered market in the village's main square, built in the 19th century, and an octagonal fountain. There are shops and a bicycle store here. One of the village's jewels is a restaurant, le Vieux Logis, housed in a medieval house in the old part of town next to one of the old gates. Vias hosts an open-air jazz festival in summer; the main events take place in the sports stadium with smaller concerts in other locations including a late night festival club.

Vias beach is a large highly developed resort. Its long sandy beach attracts visitors from northern France and northern Europe.

Continue cycling on the northern bank. Note a canal leaving the south bank after the Libron works, which leads to the Mediterranean. Pass under a road and railway bridge and shortly afterwards come to a beautiful

## STAGE 5 – BÉZIERS TO SÈTE

*Round lock in Agde*

old stone bridge. ▶ Having **crossed to the south side of the canal** the path narrows and there are exposed roots, mooring ropes and a ditch on the right. There are a number of permanent residents living in barges here – you have reached **Agde**. **The path leaves the Canal du Midi at Agde round lock.**

Cross the road to see **Agde round lock**. This is unique on the Canal du Midi system, and has three exits: to the canal towards Vias, to the Hérault river, and to a canalet that runs to Agde.

Follow the canal for 200m to where it meets the Hérault river. Boats cross the river and rejoin the canal on the other bank. The river is wide and without a bridge at this point so cyclists have to make a major detour.

From the round lock follow the road and a path beside the canalet to the town centre. The path rises to the road after 700m. Cross the road using the pedestrian crossing and then cycle across the Hérault river by way of the busy main bridge to explore the old town of Agde.

Change to the south bank.

**Agde** was an old Greek town founded long before Marseille. It sits beneath Mont St-Loup, an extinct volcano that provided the black stone from which the town was built. The fertile volcanic soil is probably what attracted the first settlers, and Marco Polo nicknamed it 'the black pearl of the Mediterranean'. In common with many towns in the region Agde was destroyed by the Vandals, the Arab armies and Charles Martel. In addition, Admiral Roger de Loria sacked the town in AD1286 and it was fought over again during the wars of religion. In more recent times, Agde provided a base for refugees from the Spanish republican army in 1939 until the arrival of Nazi troops in 1942.

The quays on the left bank (eastern side) of the river are lined with restaurants and cafés. The town's most obvious monument is St Etienne Cathedral, a massive 35m-high structure built more like a fort than a church. The altar and its backdrop are constructed from white marble. ▸

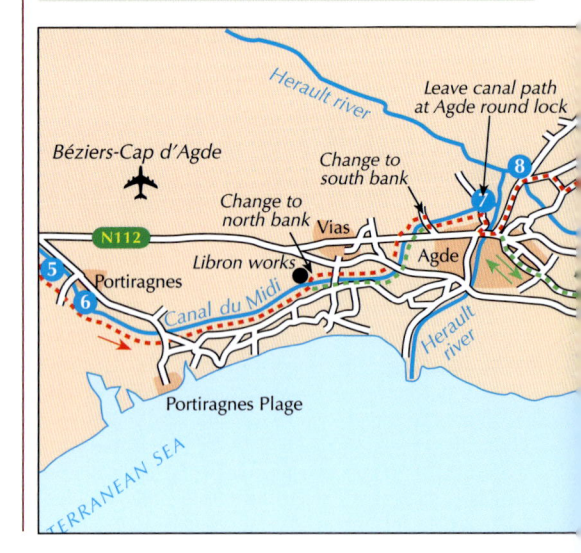

map continued from page 136

*Stage 5 – Béziers to Sète*

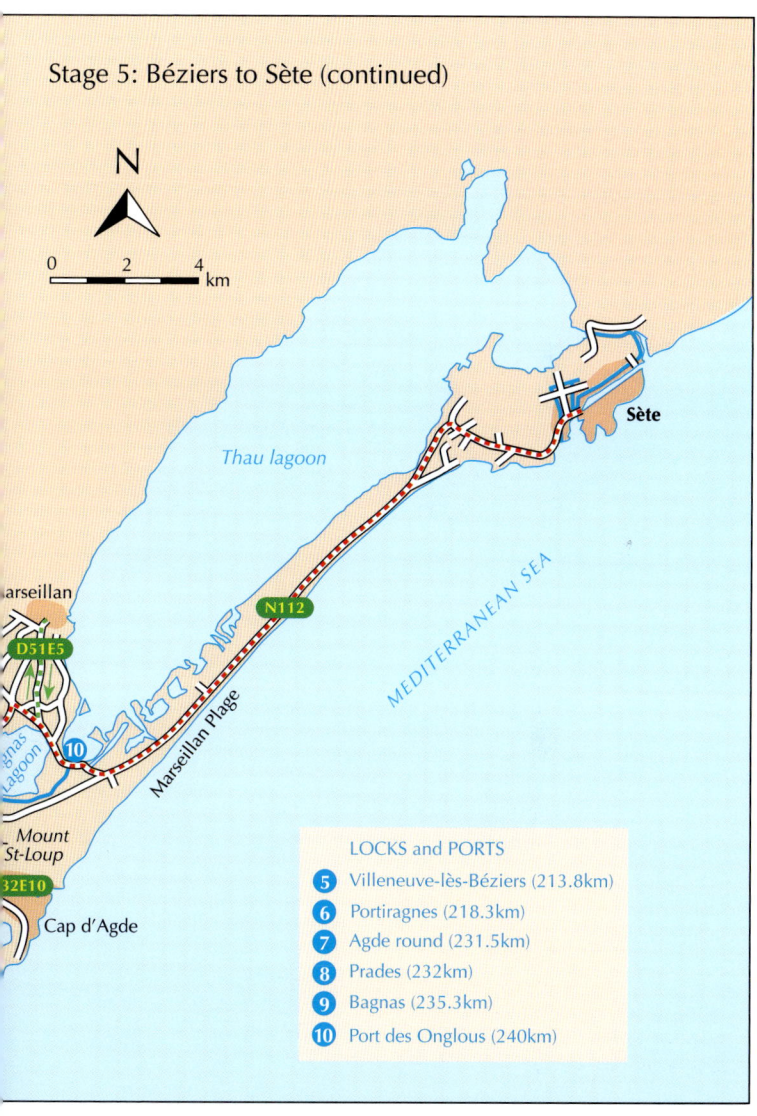

## Stage 5: Béziers to Sète (continued)

**LOCKS and PORTS**
- ⑤ Villeneuve-lès-Béziers (213.8km)
- ⑥ Portiragnes (218.3km)
- ⑦ Agde round (231.5km)
- ⑧ Prades (232km)
- ⑨ Bagnas (235.3km)
- ⑩ Port des Onglous (240km)

*Interior of Agde cathedral*

◀ Rue Honoré Muratet is the main old street in the town, and runs parallel to the river and quays. Apart from the cathedral, old houses and buildings add to the town's appeal. The Hôtel de Ville (Town Hall) and its arcades date from the 17th century. Further along the street there are signs for the Musée Agathois, the town's museum, a few paces from the main thoroughfare. The museum has displays covering the rich history of the town and the surrounding area (l'Agadès).

Agde is a renowned tourist location. Cap d'Agde is the local seaside resort, less than 5km away, and a cycle path runs beside the main road from Agde's outskirts to the port. Cap d'Agde has several fine beaches including Plage Richelieu, which is also served by a cycle track. Aqualand is one of Europe's largest water parks and is close to the port. ▶

## STAGE 5 – BÉZIERS TO SÈTE

◄ The Cap is also home to one of world's largest naturist centres, beside the eastern beach. Other attractions include the underwater archaeology museum with displays of artefacts found in the sea and nearby lagoons. The main attraction is a Greek statue of an almost naked man cast in bronze, which was found in the Hérault river in 1964. You can also follow a marked underwater trail (using snorkelling equipment). Brescou Fort is on an island just off the Cap and can be visited by boat. The fort was strategically important for the defence of the coastline until the 19th century, and was used as a prison until 1851.

### DETOUR TO MONT ST-LOUP

**Mont St-Loup** is 4km from Agde. The hill is 144m above sea level and has commanding views of the town, lagoons, Mont St-Clair, Sète, the coast and countryside.

Follow the cycle path from Agde towards **Cap d'Agde** (starting from a roundabout at the edge of town). Turn left following a sign for a campsite, Domaine de La Pinede, onto Rue de Luxembourg. Use a pedestrian crossing to get to the other side as the road is busy. Note the entrance to the hill park on the right. Go past the barrier and cycle through the pine trees to the top where you'll find the lighthouse.

From the top, you can look down on Agde. The Bagnas lagoon is to the northeast; the canal passes to the south of this, between the lagoon and a marsh of the same name, and together these form a nature reserve. This guide recommends that you don't cycle this short stretch of the canal (see below), but you get a chance to see it from the top of Mont St-Loup.

There is a roundabout shortly after crossing the bridge over the Hérault. Take the exit marked Marseillan, D51. Stay on this busy road, taking care when crossing the railway tracks at a level crossing. Continue for another 1km until reaching the canal. The towpath from here to the Bassin de Thau (**Thau lagoon**) is badly undermined and prone to subsidence, and this guide recommends an

## CYCLING THE CANAL DU MIDI

alternative route. Using the path may be dangerous and cause further erosion.

Cross the canal bridge and take a road to the right approximately 30m further on. The next part of the cycle is very exposed; make sure you wear appropriate protection against the sun. You'll see signs for a campsite. Follow the road as its swings left and take the second turn to the right (the first turn to the right is a short dead end). At the next junction take a left turn and cycle straight ahead keeping a factory-like building to your right. Take the road dropping to the right approximately 100m past the factory and marked by a stone cross on your left.

You are now cycling on a tarmac road, but this gradually degrades to a track. Note Mont St-Loup to your right and Mont St-Clair ahead in the distance. Go straight through a crossroads (tracks). The surface varies between pebbles and dust. Cycle along the northern rim of the nature reserve, Reserve Naturelle du Bagnas (**Bagnas lagoon**), a temporary home for migrating birds.

Turn right at the next crossroads to enter a 50km zone in a modern hamlet, les Mougères, a suburb of Marseillan. Turn right at the next roundabout.

### DETOUR TO MARSEILLAN

**Marseillan** is north of this route, and can be reached by cycling north on the D51E5 for 2km. The town is on the edge of the Bassin de Thau, has a small port and is a good place to buy seafood – especially oysters (the Bassin de Thau is one of France's major oyster-producing areas). Rafts used in their production can be seen floating in the lagoon. It is also close to the vineyards of Pinet, Florensac and Pomérols, which produce a dry white wine made from the Picpoul grape, Picpoul du Pinet – the perfect accompaniment to a plate of fresh oysters.

Return by the same route.

Follow the D51E5 south and cross the last bridge over the canal. It is possible to take the towpath on the left south and follow it towards the Bassin de Thau, but the

## STAGE 5 – BÉZIERS TO SÈTE

track is barred after 300m; this is a far as you can travel on the canal towpath. The lighthouse, white with a red top, can be seen at the end of the narrow strip of land that brings the towpath to the lagoon: the **Port des Onglous**. Boats cross the lagoon to Sète and then onto the Mediterranean.

Return to the main road (D51E5), turn left and continue cycling south to a roundabout (very busy in summer). Take the exit marked Sète (D612). There is a cycle path for a 200m stretch on the right. Cross a bridge (there is a cycle path to the port to your right – don't take this). The road has a wide hard shoulder and is easy to cycle. This brings you to a main road (N112) beside a 9km-long sandy beach. Take care – cars park on both sides of it during the summer – watch out for doors opening and vehicles pulling out. The dense parking is a benefit in that it slows traffic. The beach is very popular, and it is worth stopping for a swim. ▶

Continue to the end of the beach. Go straight through the first roundabout at its end. Pass through the second roundabout following a sign for Montpellier/ Centre Ville. Take the right exit, signed Centre Ville, at the third roundabout. Continue to follow signs for Centre Ville through the fourth roundabout (l'Europe) and then join the cycle path on your right. Follow this to the port, passing the Théâtre de la Mer (Theatre of the Sea). There is a pier in the port with a lighthouse at its end, from where you can look southwards towards the harbour opening.

Continue into **Sète** centre.

The authorities began work on the road from Marseillan to Sète in the summer of 2008; as a result the route may change. Follow signs for Sète if this has happened.

### Sète

Sète is known as the 'Venice of the Mediterranean', and is dominated by Mont St-Clair (175m above sea level). The Bassin de Thau is to the north and the Mediterranean to the south, linked by a canal system. **Canal de Sète** is the main waterway with the **Canal Lateral**, **Canal Maritime** and the **Darse de la Peyrade** making up the rest of the system. **The Canal du Rhône à Sète** leaves the north of the town and travels 80km to the town of Beaucaire, where it joins the River Rhône.

## CYCLING THE CANAL DU MIDI

Sète stretches along the quays on either side of the main canal. Cafés and restaurants give you the opportunity to sit and watch town life unfold. This is the main centre for the sport of water jousting, *joutes nautiques* (see Introduction). The jousts take place throughout the summer. St Peter's festival takes place in late July, the main event being a boat procession bringing the statue of the saint from St Louis church to the harbour. The statue is placed on an altar on board a trawler, and blessed. Floral decorations are scattered on the water in memory of those who have lost their lives at sea.

Sète is the birthplace of the poet Paul Valéry and the singer-songwriter Georges Brassens; both have museums named in their honour. The Paul Valéry museum is close to the port, and has archaeological displays as well as a room devoted to the poet's life. The Brassens museum concentrates on the singer's life and his influences.

**Mont St-Clair** is the town's major attraction, and can be accessed from several points in the town. From the

*The harbour in Sète*

*Journey's end*

port, follow the Promenade Maréchal-Leclerc away from the town centre and take the right fork up the Avenue du Tennis into the Park des Pierres Blanches; look back at the Bassin de Thau. Follow the path from here to **Notre Dame de la Salette**, a chapel built in the grounds of an old fort. It's a place of pilgrimage particularly on or around 19 September.

Sète is a wonderful place to end (or indeed) start a cycle. Bathed in bright light, its shops, restaurants and inhabitants welcome those who have finished their journey – and inspire those just setting out.

## EXCURSION
*to Vendres salt lagoon*

| | |
|---|---|
| **Distance** | 46 or 49km (two options) |
| **Path** | Roads, dirt track, very stony for a short stretch |
| **Shade** | Very exposed, little shade |
| **Climb** | Flat: occasional small hills (less than 20m) to reach maximum of 60m |
| **Maps** | 65 and 72 IGN *Carte de Promenade* |

This excursion brings you to the salt lake of **Vendres**. It is a beautiful and often wild environment with wonderful views over the lagoon. The lakeside provides a habitat for rare wild orchids and other flowers. The reeds and open water support a varied bird life, including flamingos.

The route passes alongside the Aude river as it approaches silver beaches and the sea, passing close to Roman ruins and an almost dry sulphur spring. **Vendres** is a small compact village, dating back at least to Roman times. Its church and associated buildings were built and redeveloped from the 13th to 17th centuries. This cycle leads to the village centre opposite the town hall; the church is reached through the small side streets. There is also a wash house behind the town hall. There are shops, a café and two restaurants in the small narrow streets, and the pizzeria does a good basic meal.

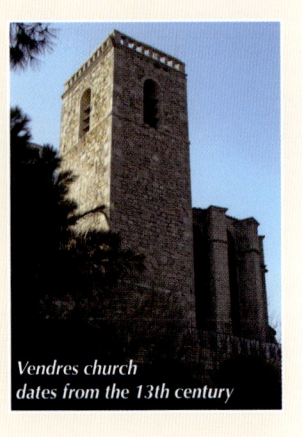

*Vendres church dates from the 13th century*

The cycle is relatively flat. The track around the lagoon is muddy and in a few places stony; the latter is difficult to cycle but can easily be walked. The route is exposed with little shelter from sun or rain, and the offshore wind is often strong. The lake circuit is just under 30km in length. This guide gives two alternative routes to reach Vendres from **Fonsérannes locks** (9km) or from **Villenueve-lès-Béziers** (10.5km).

# Excursion to Vendres salt lagoon

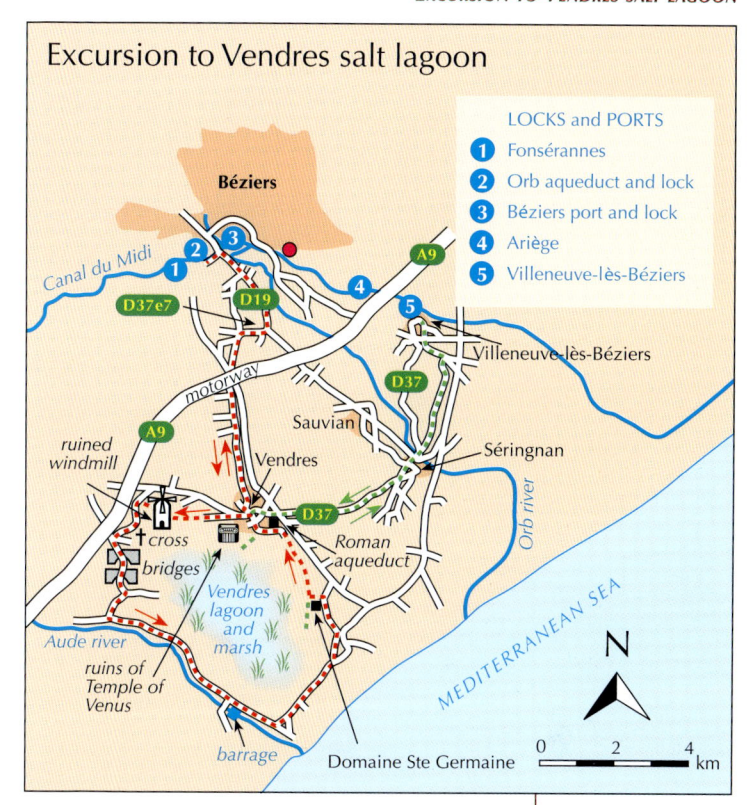

**LOCKS and PORTS**
1. Fonsérannes
2. Orb aqueduct and lock
3. Béziers port and lock
4. Ariège
5. Villeneuve-lès-Béziers

## *From Ecluse de Fonsérannes (9km)*

Cross to the south bank using the small footbridge before the canal's division into the canal to Béziers and the Canal du Midi. Descend to the left and then take the path leading to a high bridge to the right. It crosses a channel that the mechanised barge carrier uses to bypass the locks (worth viewing even if you don't want to go to the lagoon). Follow the road to the left, taking a left again when you reach the *chemin rural* (CR) 156. Reach a roundabout and turn right onto the D19. The canal aqueduct is on your left.

*Cycling the Canal du Midi*

The road goes through a series of roundabouts and reaches a T-junction 3km from the Fonséranes locks. Follow signs for **Vendres**. Turn right onto the D37e7. A further 1.5km along the road you reach a roundabout; go straight through and under a main road. Almost immediately turn right and climb to the main road. Continue on this road to the next roundabout, which should be immediately visible (motorway toll booths are on the left on the opposite side of the road) Take a small road on the right in the middle of the roundabout. Go under the motorway. This small road goes around a small building, and runs parallel to the main road just left. At a fork take the left branch and continue parallel to the main road, passing a garage and restaurant. Bear left and continue parallel to the main road.

At 7.8km reach a junction; turn right to Vendres (not Vendres Plage). Continue into the village centre along Avenue des Oliviers.

### *From Villeneuve-lès-Béziers (10.5km)*

Leave **Villeneuve-lès-Béziers** at the bridge and take the main road that enters the town. Note the modern town hall and town square on your right. At a roundabout take the road to the left for Séringnan. Pass straight through a second roundabout, still following signs for Séringnan. Take a left turn 10m later. You may see a small blue sign, circle and arrow, on the road. On your left there may also be a noticeboard and route map showing cycle tracks in the surrounding countryside.

Continue on the D37E12. Stay on the road as it bears right. At 1.5km from the bridge note a small road to the right, with stone walls on each side. The road is concrete and should be marked with a blue sign. It changes to a dirt road after 0.5km and is lined with bamboos on the left. The road gradually improves and becomes partially tarmac again. Pass an old distillery on your left complete with a tall chimney, and come to a main road.

Cross the main road and take the bridge over the Orb towards **Séringnan**. There is a roundabout at the end

*Road marking on the cycle track leaving Villeneuve-lès-Béziers for Séringnan*

of the bridge on the town side. Turn right here and within 50m turn left (following the main road), now following signs for Vendres. Pass the Cave Co-operative on your right, an award-winning wine producer; its red wines are excellent and worth trying.

Follow the road as it climbs past College Marcel Pagnol on the left. Come to a well-laid tarmac cycle path on the right as you near the top of the hill and leave the town. Join this and continue on it for 5km towards Vendres, with a good view of Béziers in the distance on your right. Cycle through vineyards past **Sauvian** airstrip (right).

Come to a large roundabout; go straight through, using the cycle paths. Come to another roundabout and pass a college on the right. Re-join the road at the tennis courts; watch out for a good view of Vendres lagoon on your left. Drop down hill into **Vendres** (signs for Centre Ville), with the church on a hill to the right.

### *Vendres lagoon circuit*

From Vendres centre take the D37 towards Lespingnan, Nissan-Lez-Ensérune, the Oppidum d'Ensérune and the Complex Sportif. Cross a bridge over a storm drain and take the left road at the fork, following the sign for the Complex Sportif. Pass the stadium (*stade*) on the right, and beside it a building that appears to be a school. The road now runs alongside the lagoon. Once past Domaine de Castelnau the road changes from tarmac to a dirt track. At a T-junction, 2km from the village, turn left towards farm buildings. Pass a partially obscured cross on the right.

Turn right at the farm buildings and join a very rough stony stretch. Those riding lighter bikes or with narrow tyres may wish to dismount and wheel their bikes. Note the remains of an old building on your left. There was once a sulphur spring here but all that seems to remain is the rotten-egg smell. Continue on the track towards pine trees; the road bears left around these. Make sure to look back at the view of the lagoon. Follow this path as it passes a house set back from the road on the right.

*View of Vendres lagoon from the remains of the Roman aqueduct*

Come to a T-junction with a tarmac road 4km from the village. Turn left in the direction of a hill with a cross on top. Pass the cross on the left and continue towards a ruined windmill, with some almond trees beside the road. It's worth pausing at the ruin to take in the view of the lagoon and the Mediterranean in the distance. The road drops quickly to join a road passing through an underpass below the A9 motorway, and with other roads forms a crossroads. Be careful as cars may come through this at speed, not expecting cyclists descending the hill towards them. There is a cross beside this crossroads. Take the second road to the left (not the one beside the cross) – this is the road that descends less steeply and is opposite the underpass road. Continue to descend on the tarmac road to reach the plain approximately 6.5km from the village centre. Cross two small bridges in quick succession (Pont de Pâtres and Pont de Eoisard).

## Excursion to Vendres salt lagoon

Reach a T-junction shortly after the bridges. Turn right, still on a small road. Come to another T junction after 1km; turn left and join the Chemin de Fleury d'Aude. You are now cycling with the Aude river on your right, although it may be masked by bamboos occasionally.

Pass a bridge with flood gates to your right (12km from Vendres). Continue straight on. Take a rough road and continue until you reach a point where there is a sign reading *Privé* (Private). Turn left. The road passes a small marina on the right.

The road merges with a main road, turning slightly to the right, and you cycle along the Avenue du Port (D37E9). Pass a bus stop for Les Sablons, staying on the road as it bends slightly to the left. Reach a large roundabout and take the exit to the left signposted for Vendres. Continue on this road, still the D37E9, climbing to reach the **Domaine Ste Germaine**. Take the small track to the left that leads down to the lagoon.

You may see a sign offering locally grown saffron for sale depending upon the time of year. The road drops and is level with the lagoon. The path to the left leads towards a good place to find wild flowers in spring and summer (do not pick these – some are rare species).

Keep a sharp look out for a rock outcrop above you on your right-hand side as you cycle towards Vendres. Look out for a small plaque (or a place where a plaque should be) beside the road, also on the right. The rocks above are the only remains of a **Roman aqueduct**. It can be accessed on foot – about 10m from the road – by way of some stone steps. Mind the cacti close to the path.

The remains of a **Roman Temple of Venus** can be found 100m further on the lake shore (towards Vendres). Look for a dirt track to the left, and follow this to the shore and the temple ruins. There is a plaque close by. You are asked to stay outside the ruins as they have yet to be fully excavated.

Re-join the track and return to the village, then retrace your route back to the canal.

*Cycling the Canal du Midi*

## EXCURSION
*across Portiragnes marshes and to Séringnan*

| | |
|---|---|
| **Distance** | 34km |
| **Path** | Tarmac cycle path, roads and dirt track |
| **Shade** | Very exposed and possibility of strong winds |
| **Climb** | Flat with few very small climbs |
| **Map** | 65 IGN *Carte de Promenade* |

This excursion starts with a visit to one of France's better Mediterranean beaches, and crosses a marsh of special scientific interest. The River Orb is followed to the beautiful town of Séringnan before visiting Sauvian village and then re-joining the canal at the Fonséstrangles locks in Béziers and returning to the start point along the canal.

> The **Camargue-like marshes** between Portiragnes and the Mediterranean are home to a diverse range of wildlife. Once part of the River Orb delta, the marshes are now managed using a series of sluice gates and dykes. The marshes flood in winter and gradually dry out in summer.
>
> Ranchers and shepherds graze cattle, horses and sheep on the exposed pastures, mainly in spring and autumn. Cowboys and cowgirls, riding Camargue-type horses, herd the traditional black longhorn cattle. Obey any warnings against entry into areas and stick to the hardened clay paths. The marshes are closed to the public when the floodgates are opened, usually in late January and most of February. Depending on the extent of the flooding the edges of the marsh can still be visited.
>
> You may see flocks of several hundred flamingos in the marsh's larger waterways. Numbers reduce in high summer as the water level drops. There are also ▸

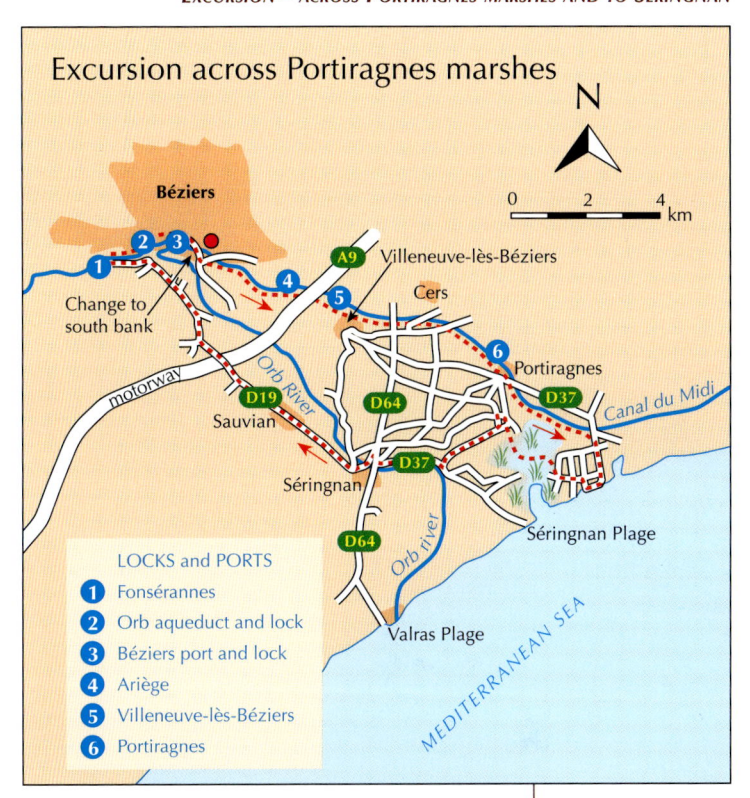

***Excursion – across Portiragnes marshes and to Séringnan***

## Excursion across Portiragnes marshes

**LOCKS and PORTS**
1. Fonsérannes
2. Orb aqueduct and lock
3. Béziers port and lock
4. Ariège
5. Villeneuve-lès-Béziers
6. Portiragnes

◀ stints, egrets, herons (purple), hoopoes, bee-eaters, kingfishers, lesser and great reed warblers, moustached warblers, great spotted cuckoos, divers and, in autumn, storks. In winter, you may spot Egyptian ibis among the flamingos, escapees from Sigean Safari Park.

Southern tree frogs thrive in the irrigation channels along with otters and coypu. From spring to late autumn, the marshes are home to many species of butterflies and moths.

*Flamingos in the Portiragnes marshes*

At the first bridge after **Portiragnes** village, in the Sète direction, follow the tarmac cycle path leading to the sea at **Portiragnes Plage**. Pass campsites on your right with a road (D37) on your left. After 200m come to a roundabout. Leave the path, which bears to the right, and join the road continuing straight on towards the sea, 1.6km from the bridge.

Follow the road, turning right, with the sea on your left. Pass cafés, a hotel and summerhouses. The beach is popular and very developed, but quieter than most other beaches in the area as it is confined by rivers and inlets at each end. In summer there are plenty of shops and restaurants open. There are morning and evening markets.

At the end of the beach promenade the road bends sharply to the right. Continue past an open space, shops and a car park (left), and you'll see a square (Place du Bicentenaire) also on your left. In season, restaurants and shops open on to it. There is a tourist office on the left towards the back of the square.

Cross the square and exit by a small road/lane. Follow this (Chemin de la Rivierette), crossing a roundabout and a

## Excursion – across Portiragnes marshes and to Séringnan

road and passing chalets and permanent tents, until you reach a T-junction close to a roundabout (left). Turn right and almost immediately take a left turn onto a mud track beside a pumping station. A notice advises you that you are now entering the marsh.

Follow this path, passing behind a set of sluice gates about 100m from the entrance. The local authority has put barriers here to stop cars going further. There are saltmarshes to the left and reedbeds to the right. Beyond the reedbeds there are open expanses of water; you can often spot flamingos and a great variety of waterfowl.

Continue on the path to a point where paths lead off in several directions. Continue straight on alongside another set of sluice gates, 1.2km from the marsh entrance. You can usually pass on either side.

The path now turns inland beside an inlet that becomes progressively reed-covered. Pass over a further two sluice gates. Approximately 80m after the second sluice gate is a noticeboard describing the wildlife found in the area (3.3km from where you entered the marsh). Turn left here and immediately cross another sluice gate

*Séringnan church and the Orb river*

163

to reach a tarmac road. Take a left turn over a small bridge and then an immediate right to cycle on a tarmac road with an irrigation channel on the right. After a little over 1km, the road surface deteriorates; note Séringnan church spire directly ahead. Turn left at the next junction, and after 500m turn right at a T-junction.

Continue on this road until you join a larger main road. Turn right. The River Orb flows alongside the road on the other side. The route passes through Séringnan's vineyards, with signs indicating the varieties of grapes growing in the different plots. After 2km pass through two busy junctions, one on either side of a bridge that you pass under.

Turn left after 250m into **Séringnan**, crossing the Orb. At the roundabout turn left towards town centre. The road leads to the central square.

---

**Séringnan** is one of the most attractive towns in the area, and benefited hugely from the growth in the wine trade in the 19th century. Wine still plays an important part in the town's life.

The town's close association with local cattle raising and horse riding is recognised in the museum of horse and harness on Avenue de la Plage. The area produces fruit and vegetables and these can be bought in the market, one of the better small open markets.

L'église Notre Dame des Graces (church of Our Lady of Grace) is the town's architectural gem. It dates back to at least AD990, although the present building is 13th century. The beautiful triple nave includes 13th-century woodwork decorated with frescos of the life of St Louis.

It is worth while pedalling around the town's narrow back streets; the old town is behind the hotel and cafés on the main square. The street names are in French and Occitan, often with different meanings. There are plenty of shops, a fishmonger and services ▶

## EXCURSION – ACROSS PORTIRAGNES MARSHES AND TO SÉRINGNAN

◀ in the centre, a large hypermarket on the outskirts and a tourist office just off the main square. It has a hotel and *chambres d'hôtes*, and campsites at Séringnan beach nearby.

Return to the roundabout at end of the bridge over the Orb. Take the road (D19) for 1.5km (often busy) to **Sauvian**, passing the municipal buildings on your right.

*The Clocktower Gate in Sauvian*

165

> **Sauvian** is an old village dating back to Gallo-Roman times. Two pillars from AD44 have been found, marking the intersection of three Roman roads. Note an archway down a small street on the right as you enter the village. This is la Port de l'Horloge (the Clocktower Gate); the gate dates from the 12th century, while the clocktower is from the 15th. The gate opens on to a small square with a 17th-century fountain. Nearby is a château built in the 12th century but rebuilt in the 18th, and the 14th-century church is worth visiting.

The route continues on the D19 northwards and crosses the A9 motorway 2.25km after Sauvian. At the next junction follow the road right (don't take the roads signed for either Vendres or Sauvian). Note a bus stop (St Martin) on this road. The aqueduct carrying the canal over the Orb river comes into view after 3km; at the roundabout before it turn left onto the CR156. Take the right fork up the Allée des Eclusiers and climb to the **Fonsérannes locks**. There is a great view of Béziers from the bridge over the channel for the mechanical barge lift. Take the footbridge to the north of the canal and return to Portiragnes Plage as described in the main text.

# APPENDIX 1
*Stage planning table*

To help you plan days of a suitable length, the table below gives the distances (in kilometres) between the main stops on the canal.

| | | | | | | | | | | | | | | | | | | |
|---|---|---|---|---|---|---|---|---|---|---|---|---|---|---|---|---|---|---|
| 251 | 233 | 227 | 218 | 215 | 207 | 200 | 194 | 188 | 173 | 166 | 147 | 140 | 127 | 105 | 79 | 65 | Toulouse | |
| 186 | 168 | 162 | 153 | 150 | 142 | 135 | 129 | 123 | 108 | 101 | 82 | 75 | 62 | 40 | 14 | Castelnaudary | | |
| 172 | 154 | 148 | 139 | 136 | 128 | 121 | 115 | 109 | 94 | 87 | 68 | 61 | 48 | 26 | Bram | | | |
| 146 | 128 | 122 | 113 | 110 | 102 | 95 | 89 | 83 | 68 | 61 | 42 | 35 | 22 | Carcassonne | | | | |
| 124 | 106 | 100 | 91 | 88 | 80 | 73 | 67 | 61 | 46 | 26 | 20 | 13 | Marseillette | | | | | |
| 111 | 93 | 87 | 78 | 75 | 67 | 60 | 54 | 48 | 33 | 26 | 7 | Laredorte | | | | | | |
| 104 | 86 | 80 | 71 | 68 | 60 | 53 | 47 | 41 | 26 | 19 | Homps | | | | | | | |
| 85 | 67 | 61 | 52 | 49 | 41 | 34 | 28 | 22 | 7 | Le Somail | | | | | | | | |
| 78 | 60 | 54 | 45 | 42 | 34 | 27 | 21 | 15 | Argeliers | | | | | | | | | |
| 63 | 45 | 39 | 30 | 27 | 19 | 12 | 6 | Capestang | | | | | | | | | | |
| 57 | 39 | 33 | 24 | 21 | 13 | 7 | Poilhès | | | | | | | | | | | |
| 51 | 33 | 27 | 18 | 15 | 8 | Colombiers | | | | | | | | | | | | |
| 44 | 26 | 20 | 11 | 3 | Béziers | | | | | | | | | | | | | |
| 36 | 18 | 12 | 3 | Villeneuve-les-Béziers | | | | | | | | | | | | | | |
| 33 | 15 | 9 | Portiragnes | | | | | | | | | | | | | | | |
| 24 | 6 | Vias | | | | | | | | | | | | | | | | |
| 18 | Agde | | | | | | | | | | | | | | | | | |
| Sète | | | | | | | | | | | | | | | | | | |

# APPENDIX 2
## Accommodation

The following is not an exhaustive list. The suggested accommodation is spaced along the canal or on the excursions to enable you to plan ahead.

Contact details include a local telephone number. To dial from abroad add the prefix 0033 and remove the first zero from the number listed.

## STAGE 1: TOULOUSE TO PORT LAURAGAIS

### Toulouse

**Hotels**

Hotel Ibis Gare Matabiau
14 Boulevard Bonrepos
31000 Toulouse
Tel: 0561625090
Email: H2772@accor.com
**www.ibishotel.com**

Hotel Mercure Matabiau
62 Boulevard Pierre Sémard
31500 Toulouse
Tel: 0534413670
Email: H1259@accor.com
**www.mercure.com**

Hotel Riquet
92 Rue Riquet
31000 Toulouse
Tel: 0561625596
Email: reception@hotelriquet.com
**www.hotelriquet.com**

Hotel Ibis Ponts Jumeaux
99 Boulevard de la Marquette
31000 Toulouse
Tel: 0562272828
Email: H1430@accor.com
**www.ibishotel.com**

Hotel Kyriad Toulouse Centre
5-7 Boulevard de la Gare
31500 Toulouse
Tel: 0561341171
Email: kyriad.toulouse.centre@lsfhotels.com
**www.kyriad.fr**

Hotel B&B Toulouse Centre
77 Boulevard de l'Embouchure
31200 Toulouse
Tel: 0892788102
Email: bb_4194@hotelbb.com
**www.hotelbb.com**

Hotel Icare
11 Boulevard Bonrepos
31000 Toulouse
Tel: 0561636655
Email: hotelicare@wanadoo.fr
**www.hotelicare.com**

Etap Hotel Toulouse Centre
27 Boulevard des Minimes
31200 Toulouse
Tel: 0892683110
**www.etaphotel.com**

## APPENDIX 2 – ACCOMMODATION

**Camping**

Camping du Pont de Rupé
21 Chemin du Pont de Rupé
31200 Toulouse
Tel: 0561700735
Email: campinglerupe31@wanadoo.fr

## Ayguesvives

**Chambres d'hôtes**

La Pradasse
39 Chemin de Toulouse
31450 Ayguesvives
Tel: 0561815596
Email: contact@lapradasse.com
**www.lapradasse.com**

**Camping**

Camping les Peupliers
RN 113
31450 Ayguesvives (Haute-Garonne)
Email: alt4347@free.fr
**www.campings-midipyrenees.com/en/camping/3747camping_les_peupliers.html**

## Villefranche-de-Lauragais

**Hotels**

Hotel de France
106 Rue de la République
31290 Villefranche-de-Lauragais
Tel: 0561816131
Email: hoteldefrancevillefranche31@wanadoo.fr
**www.hotel-de-france-villefranche.com**

Hotel Restaurant du Lauragais
15 Rue de la République
3190 Villefranche-de-Lauragais
Tel: 0561270076
Email: hoteldulauragais@wanadoo.fr
**www.hoteldulauragais.com**

## Avignonet-Lauragais

**Hotels**

L'Obélisque
2 Avenue Occitanie
31290 Avignonet-Lauragais
Tel: 0561816376

Hotel la Couchée
Port Lauragais
31290 Avignonet-Lauragais
Tel: 0561271712

**Barge/Chambres d'hôtes**

Péniche Isatis
Port Lauragais (in motorway services)
31290 Avignonet
Tel: 0534669348
Email: peniche-isatis@freesurf.fr

## STAGE 2: PORT LAURAGAIS TO CARCASSONNE

### Castelnaudary

**Hotels**

Hotel de France
2 Avenue Frédéric Mistral
11400 Castelnaudary
Tel: 0468231018
**www.hdefrance.com**

Hotel Restaurant du Centre et du Laragais
31 Cours République
11400 Castelnaudary
Tel: 0468232595
**www.hotel-centre-lauragais.com**

Hotel Restaurant la Maison du Cassoulet
24 Cours République
11400 Castelnaudary
Tel: 0468232723
**www.maisonducassolet.com**

## CYCLING THE CANAL DU MIDI

Hotel du Canal
2 ter Avenue Arnaut Vidal
11400 Castelnaudary
Tel: 0468940505

### Camping

Camping La Giraille
Chem. Fontanilles
11400 Castelnaudary
Tel: 0468941128
Email: Marie.castelnaudary@wanadoo.fr

## Villepinte

### Hotels

Hotel-Restaurant Les Deux Acacias
11150 Villepinte
Tel: 0468942467
**www.lesdeuxacacias.com**

### Camping

Camping Municipal Champ de la Rize
Chemin Montillac
11150 Villepinte
Tel: 0468942475

## Bram

### Hotels

Le Clos St Loup
69 Avenue du Razès
11150 Bram
Tel: 0468761191
Email: clos-st-loup@wanadoo.fr

Auberge Montplaisir Chez Alain
N113
11150 Bram
Tel: 0468761275
Email: auberge.montplaisir@wanadoo.fr

### Chambres d'hôtes

Chateau de la Prade
11150 Bram
Tel: 0468780399
Email: chateaulaprade@wanadoo.fr

Domaine Les Magasins
Port de Bram
11150 Bram
Tel: 0468765713
Email: relaxsud@wanadoo.fr
**www.domainelesmagasins.com**

## Pezens

### Hotels

Hotel le Réverbère
RN113
11170 Pezens
Tel: 0468249253

## Carcassonne

### Hotels

Hotel de La Cité
Place Auguste-Pierre Pont – La Cité
11000 Carcassonne
(very expensive: €275–1250)
Tel: 0468719871
Email: reservations@hoteldelacite.com
**www.hoteldelacite.com**

Hotel de L'Octroi
106 Avenue Général Leclerc
11000 Carcassonne
Tel: 0468252908
Email: hotel-octroi@ataraxie.fr

Hotel Bristol
7 Avenue Maréchal Foch
11000 Carcassonne
Tel: 0468250724
Email: hotel.bristol11@wanadoo.fr
**www.arcantis-hotels.fr**

## APPENDIX 2 – ACCOMMODATION

Hotel du Soleil le Terminus
2 Avenue du Maréchal Joffre
11000 Carcassonne
Tel: 0468252500
Email: leterminus@hotels-du-soleil.com
**www.hotels-du-soleil.com**

Au Royal Hotel
22 Boulevard Jean Jaurès
11000 Carcassonne
Tel: 0468251912
Email: godartcl@wanadoo.fr

Hotel Astoria
18 Rue Tourtel
11000 Carcassonne
Tel: 0468253138
Email: hotel-astoria@wanadoo.fr
**www.astoriacarcassonne.com**

### Chambres d'hôtes

Coté Cité
81 Rue Trivalle
11000 Carcassonne
Tel: 0468710965
Email: info@cotecite.com
**www.cotecite.com**

Au Domisiladore
19 Boulevard Marcou
11000 Carcassonne
Tel: 0468710029
Email: bodiguelj@yahoo.fr
**www.au-domisiladore.com**

Les Florentines
71 Rue Trivalle
11000 Carcassonne
Tel: 0468715107
**www.lesflorentines.net**

### Camping

Camping de la Cité Campéoles
Route de St Hilaire
11000 Carcassonne
Tel: 0468251177
Email: cpllacite@atciat.com
**www.campeoles.com**

## EXCURSION TO ST-FÉRRÉOL

### St-Martin-Lalande

#### Chambres d'hôtes

Jacqueline Delcroix
Domaine Escourrou
11400 St-Martin-Lalande
Tel: 0468949190
Email: g.delcroix@wanadoo.fr

Jacques Sabatte
La Capelle
11400 St-Martin-Lalande
Tel: 0468949190
Email: lacapelle@aol.com

### St-Papoul

#### Chambres d'hôtes

Domaine Las Brugues
Route de Lasbordes
11400 St-Papoul
Tel: 0468234311
Email: lasbrugues@hotmail.com
**www.lasbrugues.fr**

### St-Férréol

#### Hotels

Hotel La Comtadine
St-Férréol
11400 Les Brunels
Tel: 0561817303
Email: lacomtadine@wanadoo.fr
**www.lacomtadine.com**

## CYCLING THE CANAL DU MIDI

Hotel-Restaurant L'Hermitage
St-Férréol
31250 Revel
Tel: 0534661124

Hotellerie Résidence du Lac
St-Férréol
31250 Revel
Tel: 0562187080
Email: contact@hotellerie-du-lac.com
**www.hotellerie-du-lac.com**

Hotel Restaurant La Renaissance
St-Férréol
31250
Tel: 0561835150
Email: contact@hotellarenaissance.fr
**www.hotellarenaissance.fr**

### Camping

Camping En Salvan
St-Férréol le Lac
31250 Vaudreuille/Revel
Tel: 0561835595
**www.camping-ensalvan.com**

Camping Lasprades
Chemin Las Prades
St-Férréol
31250 Vaudreuille
Tel: 0561834320

## STAGE 3: CARCASSONNE TO HOMPS

### Trèbes

### Hotels

L'Andalousie
12 Rue de l'Industrie
11800 Trebes
Tel: 0468788888

Hotel la Gentilhommière
ZAC de Sautès le Bas No 6
11800 Trebes
Tel: 0468787474

### Chambres d'hôtes

La Meuniere des Forges
Pont des Forges
RN113
11800 Trèbes
Tel: 0468788513
Email: estherdreyfus13@hotmaiil.com

### Camping

Camping à l'Ombre des Micocouliers
Chemin de la Lande
11800 Trèbes
Tel: 0468786175
Email: infos@campingmicocouliers.com

## EXCURSION TO LASTOURS

### Lastours

### Camping

Camping Municipal le Belvédère
Le Belvédère
11600 Lastours
Tel: 0468775601

### Marseillette

### Hotels

Hotel la Muscadelle
67 Avenue du Languedoc
11800 Marseillette
Tel: 0468792090
Email: muscadelle@ferien-frankreich.com
**www.ferien-frankreich.com**

### Chambres d'hôtes

La Demeure la Fargue
11800 Marseillettte
Tel: 0468791388
Email: martinederoulhac@hotmail.com
**www.languedocaccueil.fr.st**

Domaine de L'horto
11800 Marseillette
Tel: 0468798014
Email: sylvainguillon@cario.fr
**www.lhorto.com**

## Puichéric

### Chambres d'hôtes

La Cime des Arbres
11700 Puicheric
Tel: 0468906226
Email: info@la-cime-des-arbes.com

Domaine les Fontanelles
11700 Puicheric
Tel: 0468437211
Email: les.fontanelles@wanadoo.fr

## Laredorte

### Chambres d'hôtes

La Marelle
19 Avenue du Minervois
11700 Laredorte
Tel: 0468915930
Email: reservations@chambres-lamarelle.com
**www.chambres-lamarelle.com**

La Closerie
Gîte and chambre d'hôtes
61 Avenue du Minervois
Laredorte
Tel: 0468906024
Email: thice1@gmail.com

## Homps

### Hotels

Auberge de l'Arbousier
50 Avenue de Carcassonne
Tel: 0468911124
Email: auberge.arbousier@wanadoo.fr

### Chambres d'hôtes

Le Relais des Chevaliers de Malta
3 Avenue du Languedoc
11200 Homps
Tel: 0670541383

Le Jardin d'Homps
21 Grand Rue
11200 Homps
Tel: 0468913950
Email: ljdh@wanadoo.fr
**www.jardinhomps.com**

En Bonne Compagnie
6 Quai des Négociants
11200 Homps
Tel: 0468912316

# EXCURSION TO MINERVE

## Olonzac

### Hotels

Hotel du Parc
Avenue de Homps
Tel: 0468913495

### Chambres d'hôtes

La Vigne Bleue
12 Rue de l'Egalité
34210 Olonzac
Tel: 0468913379
Email: sourbes.cecile@akeonet.com

## Cesseras

### Camping

Le Mas de Lignières (naturist)
Montcélèbre
F34210 Cesseras-en-Minervois
Tel: 0468912486
Email: lemas1@wanadoo.fr

## Aigne

### Chambres d'hôtes

La Maison des Causses
Rue des Causses
34210 Aigne
Tel: 0468911458
Email: contact@lamaisondescausses.com
**www.lamaisondescausses.com**

## STAGE 4: HOMPS TO BEZIERS

### Argens-Minervois

#### Chambres d'hôtes

La Bastide des Maels
18 Avenue de la Méditerranée
11200 Argens-Minervois
Tel: 0468274265
Email: bastide@domainedesmaels.com
**www.domainedesmaels.com**

La Cave
6 Rue des Muscats
11200 Argens-Minervois
Tel: 0468275573
Email: lacaveargens@wanadoo.fr

### Ventenac-en-Minervois

#### Chambres d'hôtes

La Fontenille
1 Rue du Couchant
11120 Ventenac-en-Minervois
Tel: 0468321563
Email: sundara.farley@lafontenille.org
**www.lafontenille.org**

Le Soleils Bleus
Route de Carnet
11120 Ventenac-en-Minervois
Tel: 0468432165
Email: dominique.meert@wanadoo.fr

### Le Somail

#### Hotels

Domaine Hôtelier du Somail
11120 le Somail
Tel: 0468462849
Email: gb@grandbleu.fr

#### Chambres d'hôtes

L'Aur Blan
135 Rue de la Bergerie
11120 le Somail
Tel: 0468462808
Email: aur.blan@wanadoo.fr

Le Neptune
Allée des Cyprès
11120 le Somail
Tel: 0468460474
Email: chambresleneptune@hotmail.com

### Argeliers

#### Chambres d'hôtes

Péniche La Baïsa
Le Port
11120 Argeliers
Tel: 0607881830
**www.peniche-chambreshotes.com**

## Appendix 2 – Accommodation

## Capestang

### Hotels

Le Relais Bleu
19 Cours Belfort
34310 Capestang
Tel: 0467933126

### Chambres d'hôtes

Le Mûrier Platane
34310 Capestang
Tel: 0467937845
Email: perso.wanadoo.fr/lemurielplatane

La Maison Verte
7 Rue Adolphe Saisset
34310 Capestang
Tel: 0467933853

La Bellifontaine
44 Cours Belfort
34310 Capestang
Tel: 0467933061
Email: lydie.masson@ceqetel.net
**www.bellifontaine.com**

## Poilhès

### Chambres d'hôtes

Péniche-Alegria
Boulevard Paul Riquet
34310 Poilhès
(Barge on canal – changed ownership April 2008)
**http://hotelalegria.free.fr/**

## Colombiers

### Hotels

Via Domitia
Clinique Causse – Traverse de Béziers
34440 Colombiers
Tel: 0467356263

### Camping

Les Peupliers
7 Promenade de l'Ancien Stade
Tel: 0467370526

## Béziers

### Hotels

Hotel Impérator
28 Allées Paul Riquet
34500 Béziers
Tel: 0467490225
Email: imperatorhotel@wanadoo.fr
**www.hotel-imperator.fr**

Hotel Alma
41 Rue Guilhemin
34500 Béziers
Email: reservation@hotel-alma-beziers.com
**www.hotel-alma-beziers.com**

Hotel Concorde
7 Rue Solférino
34500 Béziers
Tel: 0467283105

Hotel de France
36 Rue Boïeldieu
34500 Béziers
Email: accueil@hotel-2-france.com
**www.hotel-2-france.com**

Hotel des Poètes
80 Allées Paul Riquet
34500 Béziers
Tel: 0467763866
Email: hoteldespoetes@cegetel.net

Hotel Terminus
78 Avenue Gambetta
34500 Béziers
Tel: 0467492364
Email: contact@hotelterminus-beziers.info
**www.hotelterminus-beziers.com**

*Cycling the Canal du Midi*

### Camping

Domaine de Clairac
Route de Bessan
34500 Béziers
Tel: 0467767897
Email: camping.clairac@free.fr
**www.campingclairac.com**

## EXCURSION TO NARBONNE AND PORT LA NOUVELLE

### Sallèles d'Aude

#### Chambres d'hôtes

Les Volets Blues
43 Quai d'Alsace
11590 Sallèles d'Aude
Tel: 0468468303

Le Domaine de la Fondelon
11590 Sallèles d'Aude
Tel: 0468468707
Email: mgfondelon@aol.com
**www.lafondelon.fr**

#### Camping

Camping Municipal
Rue de la Cave Coopérative
11590 Sallèles d'Aude
Tel: 0468466846

### Narbonne

#### Hotels

Grand Hotel du Languedoc
22 Boulevard Gambetta
11100 Narbonne
Tel: 0468651474
Email: hotel.languedoc@wanadoo.fr
**www.hoteldulanguedoc.com**

Hotel la Résidence
6 Rue du 1er Mai
11100 Narbonne
Tel: 0468321941
Email: hotellaresidence@free.fr
**www.hotelresidence.fr**

Hotel de France
6 Rue Rossini
11100 Narbonne
Tel: 0468320975
Email: accueil@hotelnarbonne.com
**www.hotelnarbonne.com**

Hotel du Midi
4 Avenue de Toulouse
11100 Narbonne
Tel: 0468410462
Email: accueil@hoteldumidi.net
**www.hoteldumidi.net**

#### Chambres d'hôtes

Domaine du Petit Fidèle
Ancienne Route de Coursan
11100 Narbonne
Tel: 0468321812
Email: reservation@petitfidele.com
**www.petitfidele.com**

#### Camping

Camping Club les Mimosas
Chaussée de Mandirac
11100 Narbonne
Tel: 0468490372
Email: info@lesmimosas.fr

Camping la Nautique
11100 Narbonne
Tel: 0468904819
Email: info@campinglanautique.com
**www.campinglanautique.com**

## Port la Nouvelle

### Hotels

Hotel Méditerranée
Boulevard Front de Mer
11210 Port la Nouvelle
Tel: 0468480308
Email: hotel.mediterranee@wanadoo.fr
**www.hotelmediterranee.com**

Hotel la Rascasse
À la Plage
11210 Port la Nouvelle
Tel:0468480289

Hotel le Miramer
30 Allée des Capucines
11210 Port la Nouvelle
Tel: 0468480206

### Camping

Camping Cap du Roc
Route de La Palme
11210 Port la Nouvellle
Tel: 0468480098
Email: info@camping-cap-du-roc.com
**www.camping-cap-du-roc.com**

Camping Municipal du Golfe
Boulevard Francis Vals
11210 Port La Nouvelle
Tel: 0468480842

Camping de la Côte Vermeille
Chemin des Vignes
11210 Port la Nouvelle
Tel: 0468480580
Email: infos@camping-cote-vermeille.com
**www.camping-cote-vermeille.com**

## STAGE 5: BÉZIERS TO SÈTE

### Villeneuve-lès-Béziers

#### Hotels

Las Cigalas
28 Boulevard Gambetta
34420 Villeneuve-lès-Béziers
Tel: 0467394528
Email: info@lascigalas.com
**www.lascigalas.com**

#### Chambres d'hôtes

Viner Jennifer
7 Rue de la Fontaine
34420 Villeneuve-lès-Béziers
Tel: 0467398715
Email: anges-gardiens@wanadoo.fr

#### Camping

Les Berges du Canal
Quai du Canal
Promenade des Vernets
34420 Villeneuve-lès-Béziers
Tel: 0467393609

### Portiragnes

#### Hotels

Le Mirador
4 Boulevard Frond de Mer
Portiragnes 34420
Tel: 0467909133
**www.hotel-le-mirador.com**

#### Chambres d'hôtes

Peniche (Barge) Béatrice
Port Cassafières
34420 Portiragnes
Tel: 0603250042
Email: bateau-beatrice@wanadoo.fr
**www.bateau-beatrice.com**

### Camping

Les Sablons
Avenue des Mûriers
Plage Est
34420 Portiragnes Plage
Tel: 0467908291
**www.les-sablons.com**

Les Mimosas
Port Cassafières
34420 Portiragnes Plage
Tel: 0467909292
**www.mimosas.com**

Emeraude
Chemin du Gaillardels
34420 Portiragnes Plage
Tel: 0467909376

Familial de Vénissieux
2 Avenue des Mûriers
34420 Portiragnes Plage
Tel: 0467909244

### Vias

### Hotels

Hotel Myriam
Avenue de la Méditerranée
Vias Plage
34450 Vias
Tel: 0467216459
**www.motelmyriam.com**

Le Mucrina
Avenue du Général de Goys
34450 Vias
Tel: 0467217771
Email: contact@hotelmucrinavias.com
**www.hotelmucrinavias.com**

Hotel Gambetta
36 Boulevard Gambetta
34450 Vias
Tel: 0467216094
Email: info@hotel-legambetta.com
**www.hotel-legambetta.com**

### Chambres d'hôtes

Domaine de la Gardie
Route de Bessan
34450 Vias
Tel: 0467217922
Email: eduplan@wanadoo.fr

### Camping

La Carabasse Parc Vacance
Route de Farinette – Vias Plage
34450 Vias Plage
Tel: 0467216401
**www.lacarabasse.fr**

Californie Plage
Côte Ouest
34450 Vias
Tel: 0467216469
**www.californie-plage.fr**

Domaine de la Dragonnière
RN112
34450 Vias
Tel: 0467010310
**www.dragonniere.com**

### Agde

### Hotels

Hotel Bon Repos
15 Rue Rabelais
34300 Agde
Tel: 0467941626

## APPENDIX 2 – ACCOMMODATION

Hotel Araur
Route de Vias
Quai du Commandant Réveille
34300 Agde
Tel: 0467949777
**www.hotelaraur.com**

Le Donjon
Place Jean Jaurès
34300 Agde
Tel: 0467941232
Email: info@hotelledonjon.com
**www.hotelledonjon.com**

### Camping

La Pinède Vitalys
Rue de Luxembourg
34300 Agde
Tel: 0467212500

Les Mimosas
98 Rue Guiraudette
34300 Agde
Tel: 0467016736
**www.campingmimosas.com**

Le Coraly
Route de Sète
34300 Agde
Tel: 0467214881
**www.campinglecoraly.com**

## Sète

### Hotels

Le Grand Hotel
17 Quai Maréchal de Lattre de Tassigny
34200 Sète
Tel: 0467747177

La Joie Sables
Plage de la Corniche
Chemin des Quilles
34200 Sète
Tel: 0467531176
**www.lajoiedessables.com**

Le National
2 Rue Pons de l'Hérault
34200 Sète
Tel: 0467746785
**www.hotellenational.fr**

Les Mouettes
12 Quai de la Résistance
34200 Sète
Tel: 0467747668
Email: info@Hotel-les-Mouettes.net
**www.hotel-les-mouettes.net**

### Camping

Le Castellas
RN112
34200 Sète
Tel: 0467516300
**www.village-center.com**

## EXCURSIONS TO PORTIRAGNES MARSHES AND VENDRES

### Serignan

#### Chambres d'hôtes

Casa Belle
13 Avenue de Béziers
34410 Serignan
Tel: 0499410094
Email: casabelle34@wanadoo.fr

#### Camping (beach)

Le Clos Virigile
Serignan Plage
34410 Serignan
Tel: 0467322064
**www.leclosvirgile.com**

Le Grand Large
Aloha Village
Serignan Plage
34410 Serignan
Tel: 0467397130
**www.yellovillage-aloha.com**

Le Serignan Plage Nature
L'Orpelliere
Serignan Plage
34410 Serignan
Tel: 0467320961
**www.lesrignannature.com**

### Sauvian

#### Chambres d'hôtes

Villa Gabrielle
1 Rue des Rosiers
34410 Sauvian
Tel: 0467769153
Email: daniel-laheurte@wanadoo.fr

#### Camping

La Font Vive
11 Avenue du Stade
34410 Sauvian
Tel: 0467323316

### Vendres

#### Camping (beach)

Le Foulègues
Vendres Plage Ouest
34350 Vendres Plage
Tel: 0467373365
**www.campinglesfoulegues.com**

St Méen
Route du Grau de Vendres
34350 Vendres Plage
Tel: 0499410351
**www.camping-saint-meen.fr**

Les Mûriers
Grau de Vendres
34350 Vendres Plage
Tel: 0467326722

# APPENDIX 3
## *Tourist offices*

Most villages have a tourist office. Opening hours vary, and most are closed outside the main holiday season. The offices listed here are in the larger towns, and most are open throughout the year.

The French tourist office has a website: www.franceguide.com. The Voies Navigables de France (VNF) also has a website: www.vnf.fr.

### Toulouse
Office de Tourisme de Toulouse
Donjon du Capitole
Square Charles De Gaulle – BP 801
31080 Toulouse cedex 6
Tel: 0033 (5) 61110222
Fax: 0033 (5) 61220363
Email: infos@ot-toulouse.fr
**www.uk.toulouse-tourisme.com**

### Castelnaudary
Office de Tourisme
Place de la Republique
11400 Castelnaudary
Tel: 0033 (0) 468230573
Fax: 0033 (0) 468236140
Email: otsicastelnaudary@wanadoo.fr
**www.ville-castelnaudary.fr**

### Carcassonne
Office Municipal du Tourisme
de Carcassonne
28 Rue de Verdun
11890 Carcassonne cedex
Tel: 0033 (0) 468102430
Email: accueil@carcassonne-tourisme.com
**www.carcassonne-tourisme.com**

### Homps
Office de Tourisme
Le Chai, 35 Quai des Tonneliers
11200 Homps
Tel: 0033 (0) 468911898
Email: promotion.minervois.eur@wanadoo.fr

### Narbonne
Office de Tourisme
31 Rue Jean Jaurès
11100 Narbonne
Tel: 0033 (0) 468655912
Email: info@narbonne-tourisme.com
**www.mairie-narbonne.fr**

### Béziers
Office de Tourisme & des Congrès Béziers
29 Avenue St-Saëns
34500 Béziers
Tel: 0033 (0) 467768400
Email: tourisme@ville-beziers.fr
**www.beziers-tourisme.fr**

### Agde
Office de Tourisme
Place Molière – BP137
24302 Agde cedex
Tel: 0033 (0) 467942968
Email: ot-agde@wanadoo.fr
**www.agde-herault.com**

### Sète
Office de Tourisme
60 Grand Rue Mario Roustan
34200 Sète
Tel: 0033 (0) 467747171
Email: tourisme@ot-sete.fr
**www.ot-sete.fr**

# APPENDIX 4
*English–French glossary*

| English | French |
|---|---|
| Hello | Bonjour |
| Good evening | Bonsoir |
| Goodbye | Au revoir |
| Yes | Oui |
| No | Non |
| Please | S'il vous plaît |
| Thank you | Merci |
| I understand | Je comprends |
| I do not understand | Je ne comprends pas |
| I know | Je sais |
| I don't know | Je ne sais pas |
| I don't speak French | Je ne parle pas Français |
| Do you speak English? | Parlez-vous Anglais? |
| Watch out! | Attention! |
| Help | Aidez moi |
| I'm lost | Je suis perdu |
| I'm sick | Je suis malade |
| Where is… | Où est… |
| Toilet | Toilette |
| Do you have a room? | Avez-vous une chambre? |
| With a shower/bathroom | Avec douche/salle de bain |
| Single bed | Lit pour une personne |
| Double bed | Grand lit |
| Dish of the day | Plat du jour |
| Meal | Repas |
| Meat | Viande |
| Fish | Poisson |
| Vegetarian | Végétarien |
| Water | Eau |
| Wine (white/red) | Vin (blanc/rouge) |
| Glass | Verre |
| Tea | Thé |
| Coffee | Café |
| With milk | Au lait |

## Appendix 4 – English–French glossary

*View of Capestang from the towpath (Stage 4)*

| English | French |
|---|---|
| Turn left/right | Tournez à gauche/droit |
| Straight on | Tout droit |
| Towpath | Chemin de halage |
| Cycle track | Piste cyclable |
| Bicycle | Bicyclette, vélo |
| Brakes | Freins |
| Lock | Antivol |
| Chain | Chaîne |
| Gears | Vitesses |
| Wheel | Roue |
| Tyre | Pneu |
| Puncture | Crevaison |
| Inner tube | Chambre à l'air |
| Broken | Cassé |
| Handlebars | Guidon |
| Gloves | Gants |
| Spokes | Rayons |
| Good luck | Bon courage |
| Safe journey | Bonne route |

# APPENDIX 5
*Market days*

Most markets take place in the morning, starting early and finishing around noon. Food and clothing are usually on sale, but there are some specialist markets selling flowers, books or poultry.

### Toulouse
Markets are held every day somewhere in the city, and include:

| | |
|---|---|
| **Boulevard de Strasbourg** | (fruit and vegetables) Daily |
| **Place du Capitole** | (organic food) Tuesday and Saturday; (general and flower) Thursday |
| **Place Arnaud Bernard** | (food) Wednesday and Saturday |
| **Place du Ravelin** | (poultry and general food) Friday |
| **Place St Etienne** | (books) Saturday |
| **Rue Gatien Arnoult** | (fresh herbs) Sunday |
| **Place Jeanne d'Arc** | (flowers) Sunday |
| **Place St Aubin** | (poultry, food, clothes) Sunday |
| **Castanet** | Tuesday |
| **Villefranche-de-Lauragais** | Friday |
| **Castelnaudary** | Monday |
| **Bram** | Wednesday |
| **Carcassonne** | Tuesday, Thursday, and Saturday |
| **Trèbes** | Wednesday |
| **Narbonne** | Thursday until 4pm and Sunday morning; flower market Thursday; covered market daily |
| **Port la Nouvelle** | Wednesday and Saturday |
| **Capestang** | Wednesday and Sunday; covered market Saturday |
| **Béziers** | Friday: general (Place du 14 Juillet); flower market (Allées Paul Riquet) |

## APPENDIX 5 – MARKET DAYS

| | |
|---|---|
| **Villeneuve-lès-Béziers** | Tuesday and Saturday |
| **Portiragnes** | Sunday (summer), includes art market; Monday, Tuesday, Wednesday and Friday (July and August) at beach |
| **Vias** | (general) Saturday (all year) and Wednesday (summer); (local product market) Monday (summer) at beach; (evening artisan markets) alternate Thursdays (July and August) |
| **Agde** | Thursday |
| **Marseillan** | Tuesday in village and at beach (June to September); artisan market Friday evening (July and August) |
| **Sète** | Avenue Victor Hugo, Wednesday and Friday; Ile de Thau, Monday |

*View over Bagnas lagoon from Mt St-Loup (Stage 5)*

# APPENDIX 6
*Bike repair shops*

There are bike repair shops in most of the major towns along the route. Contact the local tourist office for more details. Bicycle repair shops are included in the local Yellow Pages directories under the heading 'Motos, scooters, cycles'. Those along the route include:

**Toulouse**
Cycles Marc
15 Allée François Verdier
31000

Louis et Cie
13 Allée Paul Feuga
31000

Atelier de Réparation du Cycle
148 Boulevard de Suisse
31200

**Carcassonne**
Cycle Raynaud
31 Boulevard de Varsovie
11000

**Trèbes**
Castilla
7 Avenue Capucins
11800

**Béziers**
Moncet Cycles
47 Avenue du Président Wilson
34500

**Vias**
Cyril Cycles
9 Place Alliés
34450

**Agde**
MBK Tomasport
12 Rue Richelieu
34300

**Sète**
Cycles Deferlantes
6 Quai Commandant Samary
34200

Midi Sports
9 Rue Languyan
34200

**Narbonne**
Cycle Cancel Alain
22 Route de Gruissan
11100 Narbonne

# APPENDIX 7
## Further reading

There are few, if any, guides in English on cycling the Canal du Midi. Several have been published in French, the most popular being *Le Canal du Midi à Vélo* by Phillipe Calas (Edisud, Aix-en-Provence, 2001). Cicerone also publish two walking guides by Alan Mattingly to the region, which contain useful information – *The Cathar Way* (Cicerone 2006) and *Walks in the Cathar Region* (Cicerone 2005).

The following books give background information on the history and culture of the region and of France.

### Cathars

*The Perfect Heresy – the life and death of the Cathars* Stephen O'Shea (Profile Books, 2000)

*The Cathars* (multiple authors) (In Situ, 2006)

*The Yellow Cross – The story of the last Cathars 1290–1329* René Weiss (Penguin, 2000)

*Labyrinth* Kate Mosse (GP Putman, 2006)
A historical novel based in Carcassonne in Cathar times and the present.

### Life in the region

*Virgile's Vinyard – a year in the Languedoc wine country* Patrick Moon (John Murray Publishers, 2003)

### French history

*A Concise History of France* Roger Price (Cambridge University Press, 2nd ed. 2006)

# SAVE £££'s with

**tgo**
THE GREAT OUTDOORS

Britain's leading monthly magazine for the dedicated walker. To find out how much you can save by subscribing call

# 0141 302 7744

**HILLWALKING · BACKPACKING · TREKKING · SCRAMBLING**

# Get ready for take off

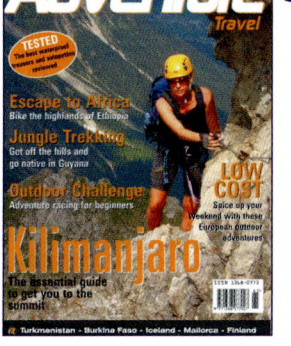

**Adventure Travel helps you to go outdoors over there**

More ideas, information, advice and entertaining features on overseas trekking, walking and backpacking than any other magazine - guaranteed.

**Available from good newsagents or by subscription - 6 issues £15**

**Adventure Travel Magazine T:01789-488166**

# LISTING OF CICERONE GUIDES

**BACKPACKING AND CHALLENGE WALKING**
Backpacker's Britain:
  Vol 1 – Northern England
  Vol 2 – Wales
  Vol 3 – Northern Scotland
  Vol 4 – Central & Southern Scottish Highlands
Book of the Bivvy
End to End Trail
The National Trails
Three Peaks, Ten Tors

**BRITISH CYCLING**
Border Country Cycle Routes
Cumbria Cycle Way
Lancashire Cycle Way
Lands End to John O'Groats
Rural Rides:
  No 1 – West Surrey
  No 2 – East Surrey
South Lakeland Cycle Rides

**PEAK DISTRICT AND DERBYSHIRE**
High Peak Walks
Historic Walks in Derbyshire
The Star Family Walks – The Peak District & South Yorkshire
White Peak Walks:
  The Northern Dales
  The Southern Dales

**MOUNTAINS OF ENGLAND AND WALES** FOR COLLECTORS OF SUMMITS
Mountains of England & Wales:
  Vol 1 – Wales
  Vol 2 – England
Relative Heights of Britain

**IRELAND**
Irish Coast to Coast Walk
Irish Coastal Walks
Mountains of Ireland

**THE ISLE OF MAN**
Isle of Man Coastal Path
Walking on the Isle of Man

**LAKE DISTRICT AND MORECAMBE BAY**
Atlas of the English Lakes
Coniston Copper Mines
Cumbria Coastal Way
Cumbria Way and Allerdale Ramble
Great Mountain Days in the Lake District
Lake District Anglers' Guide
Lake District Winter Climbs
Lakeland Fellranger:
  The Central Fells
  The Mid-Western Fells
  The Near-Eastern Fells
  The Southern Fells
Roads and Tracks of the Lake District
Rocky Rambler's Wild Walks
Scrambles in the Lake District:
  North
  South

Short Walks in Lakeland:
  Book 1 – South Lakeland
  Book 2 – North Lakeland
  Book 3 – West Lakeland
Tarns of Lakeland:
  Vol 1 – West
  Vol 2 – East
Tour of the Lake District
Walks in Silverdale and Arnside

**THE MIDLANDS**
Cotswold Way

**NORTHERN ENGLAND LONG-DISTANCE TRAILS**
Dales Way
Hadrian's Wall Path
Northern Coast to Coast Walk
Pennine Way
Teesdale Way

**NORTH-WEST ENGLAND OUTSIDE THE LAKE DISTRICT**
Family Walks in the Forest of Bowland
Historic Walks in Cheshire
Ribble Way
Walking in the Forest of Bowland and Pendle
Walking in Lancashire
Walks in Lancashire Witch Country
Walks in Ribble Country

**PENNINES AND NORTH-EAST ENGLAND**
Cleveland Way and Yorkshire Wolds Way
Historic Walks in North Yorkshire
North York Moors
The Canoeist's Guide to the North-East
The Spirit of Hadrian's Wall
Yorkshire Dales – South and West
Walking in County Durham
Walking in Northumberland
Walking in the South Pennines
Walks in Dales Country
Walks in the Yorkshire Dales
Walks on the North York Moors: Books 1 and 2
Waterfall Walks – Teesdale and High Pennines
Yorkshire Dales Angler's Guide

**SCOTLAND**
Ben Nevis and Glen Coe
Border Country
Border Pubs and Inns
Central Highlands
Great Glen Way
Isle of Skye
North to the Cape
Lowther Hills
Pentland Hills
Scotland's Far North
Scotland's Far West
Scotland's Mountain Ridges

Scottish Glens:
  2 – Atholl Glens
  3 – Glens of Rannoch
  4 – Glens of Trossach
  5 – Glens of Argyll
  6 – The Great Glen
Scrambles in Lochaber
Southern Upland Way
Walking in the Cairngorms
Walking in the Hebrides
Walking in the Ochils, Campsie Fells and Lomond Hills
Walking on the Isle of Arran
Walking on the Orkney and Shetland Isles
Walking the Galloway Hills
Walking the Munros:
  Vol 1 – Southern, Central & Western
  Vol 2 – Northern and Cairngorms
West Highland Way
Winter Climbs – Ben Nevis and Glencoe
Winter Climbs in the Cairngorms

**SOUTHERN ENGLAND**
Channel Island Walks
Exmoor and the Quantocks
Greater Ridgeway
Lea Valley Walk
London – The Definitive Walking Guide
North Downs Way
South Downs Way
South West Coast Path
Thames Path
Walker's Guide to the Isle of Wight
Walking in Bedfordshire
Walking in Berkshire
Walking in Buckinghamshire
Walking in Kent
Walking in Somerset
Walking in Sussex
Walking in the Isles of Scilly
Walking in the Thames Valley
Walking on Dartmoor

**WALES AND THE WELSH BORDERS**
Ascent of Snowdon
Glyndwr's Way
Hillwalking in Snowdonia
Hillwalking in Wales:
  Vols 1 and 2
Lleyn Peninsula Coastal Path
Offa's Dyke Path
Pembrokeshire Coastal Path
Ridges of Snowdonia
Scrambles in Snowdonia
Shropshire Hills
Spirit Paths of Wales
Walking in Pembrokeshire
Welsh Winter Climbs

## AFRICA
Climbing in the Moroccan Anti-Atlas
Kilimanjaro – A Complete Trekker's Guide
Trekking in the Atlas Mountains

## THE ALPS
100 Hut Walks in the Alps
Across the Eastern Alps: The E5
Alpine Points of View
Alpine Ski Mountaineering:
　Vol 1 – Western Alps
　Vol 2 – Central & Eastern Alps
Chamonix to Zermatt
Snowshoeing: Techniques and Routes in the Western Alps
Tour of Mont Blanc
Tour of Monte Rosa
Tour of the Matterhorn
Walking in the Alps

## EASTERN EUROPE
High Tatras
Mountains of Romania
Walking in Hungary

## FRANCE, BELGIUM AND LUXEMBOURG
Cathar Way
Écrins National Park
GR5 Trail
GR20: Corsica
Mont Blanc Walks
Robert Louis Stevenson Trail
Selected Rock Climbs in Belgium and Luxembourg
Tour of the Oisans: The GR54
Tour of the Vanoise
Trekking in the Vosges and Jura
Vanoise Ski Touring
Walking in Provence
Walking in the Cathar Region
Walking in the Cevennes
Walking in the Dordogne
Walking in the Haute Savoie:
　Vol 1 – North
　Vol 2 – South
Walking in the Languedoc
Walking in the Tarentaise and Beaufortain Alps
Walking on Corsica
Walks in Volcano Country

## FRANCE AND SPAIN
Canyoning in Southern Europe
Way of St James – France
Way of St James – Spain

## GERMANY AND AUSTRIA
Germany's Romantic Road
King Ludwig Way
Klettersteig – Scrambles in Northern Limestone Alps
Trekking in the Stubai Alps
Trekking in the Zillertal Alps
Walking in the Bavarian Alps
Walking in the Harz Mountains
Walking in the Salzkammergut
Walking the River Rhine Trail

## HIMALAYA
Annapurna: A Trekker's Guide
Bhutan
Everest: A Trekker's Guide
Garhwal & Kumaon: A Trekker's and Visitor's Guide
Kangchenjunga: A Trekker's Guide
Langtang with Gosainkund and Helambu: A Trekker's Guide
Manaslu: A Trekker's Guide
Mount Kailash Trek

## ITALY
Central Apennines of Italy
Gran Paradiso
Italian Rock
Shorter Walks in the Dolomites
Through the Italian Alps: The GTA
Trekking in the Apennines
Treks in the Dolomites
Via Ferratas of the Italian Dolomites:
　Vols 1 and 2
Walking in Sicily
Walking in the Central Italian Alps
Walking in the Dolomites
Walking in Tuscany

## MEDITERRANEAN
High Mountains of Crete
Jordan – Walks, Treks, Caves, Climbs and Canyons
Mountains of Greece
The Ala Dag (Turkey)
Treks and Climbs Wadi Rum, Jordan
Walking in Malta
Western Crete

## NORTH AMERICA
Grand Canyon with Bryce and Zion Canyons
John Muir Trail
Walking in British Columbia

## THE PYRENEES
GR10 Trail: Through the French Pyrenees
Mountains of Andorra
Rock Climbs in the Pyrenees
Pyrenees – World's Mountain Range Guide
Through the Spanish Pyrenees: GR11
Walks and Climbs in the Pyrenees

## SCANDINAVIA
Pilgrim Road to Nidaros (St Olav's Way)
Walking in Norway

## SLOVENIA, CROATIA AND MONTENEGRO
Julian Alps of Slovenia
Mountains of Montenegro
Walking in Croatia

## SOUTH AMERICA
Aconcagua

## SPAIN AND PORTUGAL
Costa Blanca Walks:
　Vol 1 – West
　Vol 2 – East
Mountains of Central Spain
Picos de Europa
Via de la Plata (Seville to Santiago)
Walking in Madeira
Walking in Mallorca
Walking in the Algarve
Walking in the Canary Islands:
　Vol 1 – West
　Vol 2 – East
Walking in the Cordillera Cantabrica
Walking in the Sierra Nevada
Walking the GR7 in Andalucia

## SWITZERLAND
Alpine Pass Route
Bernese Alps
Central Switzerland
Tour of the Jungfrau Region
Walking in the Valais
Walking in Ticino
Walks in the Engadine

## INTERNATIONAL CYCLING
Cycle Touring in France
Cycle Touring in Spain
Cycle Touring in Switzerland
Cycling in the French Alps
Cycling the River Loire – The Way of St Martin
Danube Cycle Way
Way of St James – Le Puy to Santiago

## MINI GUIDES
Avalanche!
First Aid and Wilderness Medicine
Navigating with GPS
Navigation
Snow

## TECHNIQUES AND EDUCATION
Beyond Adventure
Map and Compass
Mountain Weather
Moveable Feasts
Outdoor Photography
Rock Climbing
Snow and Ice
Sport Climbing
The Adventure Alternative
The Hillwalker's Guide to Mountaineering
The Hillwalker's Manual

For full and up-to-date information on our ever-expanding list of guides, please visit our website:
**www.cicerone.co.uk**.

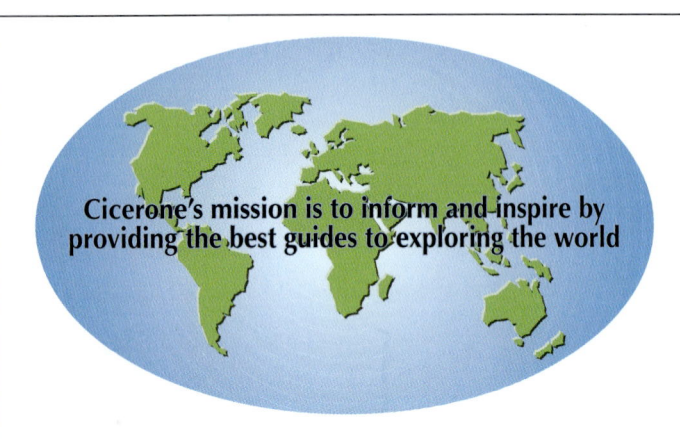

**Cicerone's mission is to inform and inspire by providing the best guides to exploring the world**

Since its foundation 40 years ago, Cicerone has specialised in publishing guidebooks and has built a reputation for quality and reliability. It now publishes nearly 300 guides to the major destinations for outdoor enthusiasts, including Europe, UK and the rest of the world.

Written by leading and committed specialists, Cicerone guides are recognised as the most authoritative. They are full of information, maps and illustrations so that the user can plan and complete a successful and safe trip or expedition – be it a long face climb, a walk over Lakeland fells, an alpine cycling tour, a Himalayan trek or a ramble in the countryside.

With a thorough introduction to assist planning, clear diagrams, maps and colour photographs to illustrate the terrain and route, and accurate and detailed text, Cicerone guides are designed for ease of use and access to the information.

If the facts on the ground change, or there is any aspect of a guide that you think we can improve, we are always delighted to hear from you.

**Cicerone Press**
2 Police Square  Milnthorpe  Cumbria  LA7 7PY
Tel: 015395 62069  Fax: 015395 63417
info@cicerone.co.uk  www.cicerone.co.uk

# CICERONE